John R. Day
A.M.Inst.T., Assoc., I.R.S.E.

Trains

illustrated by David A. Warner
& Nigel W. Hearn

TREASURE PRESS

FOREWORD

This book tries to show something of how the railways were born and grew to their present state, the work they can do today, the way they do it, and the shape they may take in the future. Railways and trains, like lorries and cars and roads, ships and the sea, aircraft and the air, are means of transport. Though some people may love them for the shape of a locomotive boiler or the carving on an old station wall, railways will only survive if they continue to earn their living. The author believes they *will* survive, even if they are so transformed as scarcely to be recognizable as the same railways which laid the foundation of the prosperity of Victorian Britain and which his family served for more than a century.

The illustrations for this book have been based partly on photographic and other material gathered by the author over a long period and partly on material newly supplied to the publisher and artist. We acknowledge here the help given us by railway administrations and railway suppliers in the preparation of this book. The author thanks them also for their general assistance over many years.

John R. Day

First published in Great Britain in 1969 by
The Hamlyn Publishing Group Limited

This edition published in 1989 by
Treasure Press
Michelin House
81 Fulham Road
London SW3 6RB

ISBN 1 85051 447 X

Printed in Yugoslavia by Mladinska Knjiga.

CONTENTS

4   How and Why the Railways Came

15   The Railways Take Over

24   The Railway Age

34   Trains for People

44   Trains for Freight

54   Tracks for Trains

65   Train Safety

74   Tractive Power for Trains

88   Handling Passengers

100   Handling Freight

112   Trains for Towns

124   The Rail Way Ahead

134   Trains for Special Jobs

146   The Future – Trains Without Rails?

156   Museums to Visit

157   Books to Read

158   Index

How and Why the Railways Came

I think you will live to see the day when railways will supersede almost all other methods of conveyance in this country – when mail coaches will go by railway and rail-roads will become the great highway for the King and all his subjects.

GEORGE STEPHENSON IN 1825

No one knows just how – or when – the first railway was built. Like the wheel, its origins are lost in the long perspective of time. Perhaps the parallel lines of grooved stone blocks laid by the Greeks to move ships across the Isthmus of Corinth some 2,500 years ago were the first railways. They were a special form of road for a special type of vehicle, they were self-guiding and permanent, and they moved both people and goods.

For our purposes we have to look back some 400 years to the days of the first Queen Elizabeth. At that time we know that men in Alsace were moving coal from the mine faces of Leberthal in small trucks with flanged wheels running on timber rails. Such a wagon, from a Transylvanian gold mine,

Loaded coal wagon coasting downhill. The horse will haul it back.

4

Early 'horse locomotive' with the horse turning a treadmill.

with a piece of track and even points, is still preserved in the Verkehrs und Bau Museum in Berlin.

The mines of northern England brought the railways to Great Britain – almost certainly before the sixteenth century was over. The mine railways spread, and in 1676 Roger North was able to describe how coal was carried from the mines to the rivers by 'bulky carts . . . made with four rowlets fitting these rails'. On these straight and parallel tracks of timber, he explained, one horse could 'draw four or five chaldrons of coals'.

This was the true secret of the rails, a secret which they still hold and keep to this day, that on them a given tractive force can do far more work than it could on any non-specialized road.

Wooden rails wore out quickly, so that when iron became cheaper and more easily worked it was natural that cast plates should be nailed over the rails to make them last longer. Angle plates were laid at Sheffield in 1776, with the wheels running on the flat part and the raised angle preventing the wheels from leaving the track. Any ordinary cart with suitable wheel spacing could use these tracks, and as the usual spacing was a little less than five feet this became standard. In this manner grew up the 'standard' gauge of 4 feet $8\frac{1}{2}$ inches used by

British Railways and by many others throughout the world.

The first rails resembling those of today came in 1789, when William Jessop, engineer of a line near Loughborough, laid his own design of cast iron rails. These first rails were very short – about three feet each – and easily broken, but they were the model from which the rails of today have grown.

When the Surrey Iron Railway, the first public freight railway in the world to be sanctioned by Parliament, opened in 1803 a test was made to see how much a single horse could draw. It was started off with twelve wagons each weighing three tons and other wagons were added at each stop. At the end of the six-mile journey the horse was pulling a fifty-five-ton train with fifty people on top of the load.

The speed of a horse walking over the sleepers between the rails was not very high, so the idea was born that the horse might be carried in the train while at the same time driving it through a form of treadmill. The first 'horse locomotives' of any practical value appeared just at the time when the steam locomotive was proving its spurs and one of them, the *Cycloped*, patented by Thomas Shaw Brandreth, was a direct competitor of the *Rocket* at the Rainhill trials in 1829. This machine had two horses but seems to have been too crudely built to give the horses a fair chance.

A better impression can be gained from trials on the South Carolina Railroad in the U.S.A. in 1830. Using a horse which the *Charleston Courier* described as 'very inferior in action and power', a twelve-passenger car built by Messrs Dotterer & Detmold ran $2\frac{1}{2}$ miles at just over 9 m.p.h. and back again at over 12 m.p.h.

Even in the 1850s, when the steam locomotive had a firm hold, an intricate, geared, horse locomotive was demonstrated in Britain, France and Germany. A two-horse version hauled

A horse-hauled train in the 1820s.

Early railway sailing car on the Baltimore & Ohio Railroad

Richard Trevithick's *Catch-me-who-can* near Euston Road.

thirty wagons in trials at Nine Elms, London, in 1850 and a four-horse type was shown in Berlin in 1853.

An even cheaper – if less reliable – method of propelling trains was tried in the U.S.A. in 1830. The Baltimore & Ohio's sailing car *Aeolus* made its maiden voyage in 1830 in charge of a sailing-master from Chesapeake Bay. Four days later she set off again carrying the eminent engineer De Witt Clinton. With a good breeze she glided along at a spanking pace, but when they came to the end of the track the sailing-master forgot to

apply the brakes, and charged into a bank of earth. The South Carolina tried a sailing car two months later. Loaded with three tons of iron ballast and fifteen people, it was dismasted by a gust of wind when making nearly twelve knots on its trial run.

The first steam locomotive to haul a load along a railway came in 1804. It was the work of a remarkable Cornishman, Richard Trevithick, who had built and demonstrated a steam road engine – known locally as 'Captain Dick's Puffer' – three years before and had designed a locomotive for the Coalbrookdale Iron Works in 1803. This locomotive was never built, but the 1804 machine was probably very like it, with one large cylinder and a huge flywheel. It had no flanges on its four wheels, for it ran on the nine-mile flanged plateway at the Penydarren Iron Works where it easily hauled a twenty-five-ton load. Another locomotive built by Trevithick, with a millwright named John Steele, in 1805 for Wylam Colliery had flanged wheels to run on wooden rails.

In 1808 Trevithick made his mark in London with a neat little eight-ton locomotive which he put to work on a circular track of iron rails in an enclosure near the present Euston Square. For a shilling the public could watch or ride in a converted barouche drawn – at up to 12 m.p.h. – by the engine. The engine was labelled 'Catch-me-who-can', and thousands did catch it until a rail broke and the locomotive overturned,

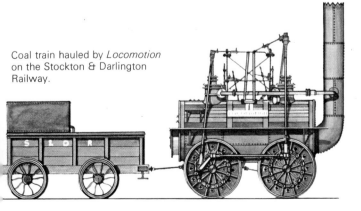

Coal train hauled by *Locomotion* on the Stockton & Darlington Railway.

ending the career of London's first steam railway and of Trevithick's interest in the locomotive. He was the true father of the locomotive, pioneering such features as the use of high-pressure steam, the turning of the exhaust steam into the chimney to improve the draught in the fire-box, and the return flue boiler. He also demonstrated that smooth wheels would haul a load on a smooth track.

George Stephenson, born at Wylam in 1781 and struggling against poverty even when made enginewright at Killingworth colliery at the age of thirty-one, asked for permission and funds and built an edge-rail locomotive with smooth wheels for

The Stephenson *Rocket*, victor of the Rainhill locomotive trials.

The age of steam arrives. Trains like these were to open up travel for all in the next few decades.

Killingworth, the first smooth wheel engine to run on iron edge-rails. Other successful Stephenson locomotives followed until, with the *Locomotion*, he brought steam to a public railway.

George Stephenson was appointed Engineer of the Stockton & Darlington Railway in 1822, and an Act of 1823 gave the railway powers both to carry passengers and to use steam locomotives. For the opening on 27 September 1825, George Stephenson and his son Robert built the four-wheeled, eight-ton *Locomotion*. According to contemporary accounts, the ninety-ton inaugural train, with George Stephenson on the footplate, reached 15 m.p.h. After the opening day the Stockton & Darlington used horses for passenger trains and kept the locomotives for coal traffic.

In the next few years locomotives were built by the Stephensons, Timothy Hackworth, Robert Wilson and others, but the great flowering of the steam age came in 1830.

After a survey of existing railways, the directors of the Liverpool & Manchester Railway, then under construction, offered a prize of £500 for the best locomotive engine to meet laid-down conditions. Five machines were ready for the trials when they began on 6 October 1829. Timothy Burstall's *Perseverance* and the *Cycloped* (already mentioned) failed to reach the required speed and Timothy Hackworth's *Sans Pareil* was over the weight limit. This left the *Rocket* and Braithwaite and Ericsson's *Novelty*, the popular favourite

11

which broke down on both days of its trials. The *Rocket*, by George and Robert Stephenson and Henry Booth, survived all the tests and reached 24·1 m.p.h. with full load, as well as 29 m.p.h. running light. It was awarded the prize and, more important, ensured that steam would work the new railway.

On 15 September 1830, the railway era began with the opening of the Liverpool & Manchester by the Duke of Wellington – the first public railway in the world to be worked entirely by steam locomotives. The glory of the occasion was marred by the first accident on a public railway, when William Huskisson, a Member of Parliament for Liverpool and a good friend of the railway, was run

The *Best Friend of Charleston*, 1830.

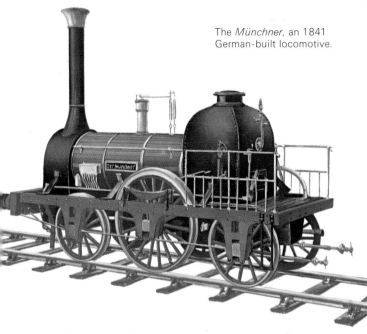

The *Münchner*, an 1841 German-built locomotive.

down by the *Rocket*. He died the same night. So began the Railway Age in mingled sacrifice and splendour.

Meanwhile, engineers elsewhere were following up, sometimes quite independently, the lead established in Great Britain. America's first steam railway was a circular track built on the lawn of Colonel John Stevens' house in Hoboken, New Jersey, on which in 1825 ran a small locomotive built by the seventy-five-year-old Colonel. Next came the *Stourbridge Lion*, imported from England in 1829, and in August 1830 the *Tom Thumb*, built by Peter Cooper of New York. The first steam locomotive to run in regular service in the U.S.A. was the *Best Friend of Charleston* on the South Carolina Railroad in 1830.

Marc Seguin built the first French locomotive in 1829, and in Germany, the first public railway was opened in 1835 between Nuremberg and Fürth. Its only locomotive came from the Robert Stephenson works. The *Beuth*, designed and built by August Borsig in Berlin in 1841, was one of the first, and in the same year the Maffei works built its first *Münchner*.

Building the early railways.
Civil engineers took on new and
gigantic tasks.

14

The Railways Take Over

Even before the Stockton & Darlington was built, William James, a land agent and surveyor, had summed up the possibilities of railways and was advocating their construction on a large scale. He and Thomas Gray of Nottingham, who asked 'Why are not these tramroads laid down all over England, so as to supersede our common roads!' already had the picture of the flowering of railways that was to succeed the opening of the Liverpool & Manchester.

In 1823 William James suggested, and made his own survey of, a railway from Canterbury to Whitstable, but it was Stephenson who was called in when the idea was adopted and his pupil John Dixon who made the final survey. The line was built by another Stephenson pupil, Joseph Locke. It also had a Stephenson locomotive – the *Invicta* – which was driven by a mechanic, Edward Fletcher, from the Stephenson locomotive works at Newcastle.

The influence of Stephenson was already considerable, but there was a time in the 1820s when he stood almost alone in his championship of locomotive haulage. The Liverpool & Manchester changed all that, and a spate of important railway bills came before Parliament as fast as schemes could be prepared. The building of these was nearly all in the hands of the Stephenson stable, with George Stephenson tackling the Grand Junction Railway (to link the Liverpool & Manchester with Birmingham) and Robert the London & Birmingham, both authorized in 1833; Joseph Locke took the London & Southampton, authorized the following year.

These works demanded large numbers of men, and the task of providing them brought forth a new race of contractors of whom Thomas Brassey was the most famous. The railways were the greatest engineering tasks since the canals, and the brawny men who did the digging were called, after the canal builders, the 'navigators', shortened to 'navvies' in later years.

Another of the important lines authorized in the early 1830s was the Great Western (1835). The engineer appointed for this railway was Isambard Kingdom Brunel, son of Sir Marc Brunel, a refugee from the French Revolution who had built the first tunnel for public traffic under the Thames and invented a tunnelling shield which, adapted by later hands, was to make the London Tube railways – and many other deep tunnels – possible.

The younger Brunel was not satisfied with the 4 foot 8½ inches gauge which Stephenson's influence had caused to be adopted elsewhere. He advocated a seven-foot gauge to allow bigger and more stable locomotives, carriages and wagons, and to this gauge the Great Western was built. He was not a locomotive man, as were the all-rounders of the Stephenson camp, and he left the designs to the firms from whom engines were ordered, so that there was little uniformity until Daniel Gooch, engaged in 1837 at the age of twenty to take charge of the motive power department, could design his own engines. The first of these, delivered in 1840, ran at 58 m.p.h. In ten years great progress had been made.

The 7 foot and 4 foot 8½ inch gauges met at Gloucester, and arrangements for transferring goods are said to have been chaotic. When Richard Cobden pressed the gauge question in Parliament a Gauge Commission was appointed. After hearing all the evidence and attending trials of rival systems, the

The excitement of early railways:
this one is in Germany.

Commission declared in 1846 for 4 foot 8½ inches as the standard gauge. The broad gauge, though it lingered for many years, began to die from then on.

The 1830s produced also George Hudson, the 'Railway King' the acme of railway promoters. He was a York draper who met George Stephenson – and impressed him – in 1835. He invested a legacy in the York & North Midland Railway and induced Stephenson to do the same. By paying dividends from capital he earned a reputation – there is still controversy over whether it was deserved – as a fine railway chairman, and was invited to join the boards of other companies. In this way he founded an empire of railway companies, forming new ones and taking over and amalgamating others on a great scale.

The growth of the railways could be described as reasonable until 1844. By then there were nearly 2,240 miles of working railway in Britain and in 1845 Gladstone established an Advisory Board to examine every new railway scheme and its promoters. Strong opposition ended the Board's work in mid-1845 and there was an immediate rush of schemes good and bad. Parliament authorized 2,170 miles of railway that

East meets West. The Union Pacific and Central Pacific meet at Promontory, Utah in 1869.

The first Pullman cars introduced in Britain in the 1870s were American in appearance and design.

year. The Railway Mania was on. Parliament was impossibly overwhelmed with railway bills – more than 470 were being considered early in April 1846 and 272 acts were passed in that year. Very often there was no money to build the authorized lines, and some promoters obtained acts only to keep others out of 'their' territory. Of the lines authorized in 1846 more than 4,500 miles were built (including some lines in Ireland), but the failure of many companies and the collapse of many railway shares brought sense to promoters and investors alike. In 1847 only 1,300 miles of line were authorized. The 1850s were largely devoted to building and linking railways already in hand, but a new upsurge of activity began in the 1860s, in which 4,500 miles of railway were added.

In the U.S.A. a number of short railways for local industrial purposes, built of wood and powered by horses, were built from 1795 onwards. The first incorporated railway – the first plateway in America – was opened on 7 October 1826. It carried granite blocks from Quincy to Milton, on the Neponset River. The first common carrier railway was the Baltimore & Ohio, opened on 24 May 1830 between Baltimore and Ellicott's Mills, thirteen miles away, with horse traction. The first steam railway was the South Carolina Railroad, which began regular services on 25 December 1830.

Expansion was rapid. Washington was linked to Baltimore by 1835 and Boston to Buffalo (except for the Hudson River crossing) by 1842. The Hudson River and the Great Lakes were linked by railway in 1851 and Chicago, which had its own local line as early as 1836, was linked by rail to the East coast by 1850 and to the Mississippi by 1854. In the West the Sacramento Valley Railroad opened in 1856, running inland from Sacramento which was linked by steamboat with San Francisco.

Because the lack of communication discouraged settlers from penetrating the West and South, the U.S.A. Federal Government offered land grants to railways from 1850, the first being to the Illinois Central Railroad. From 2,800 miles of railway in 1840, the U.S.A. systems grew to 9,000 miles in 1850, 30,000 in 1860, and 53,000 in 1870. Railway empires and emperors sprang up and prospered. Many of the lines were lightly laid over flat, easy land, with bogie locomotives and vehicles used to spread the weight over more wheels, but the distance over which the rails spread is astonishing. The long runs meant that there had to be facilities for moving about in the train, for eating and sleeping, so the open car with end platforms became the rule and George Mortimer Pullman had produced a sleeping car conversion by 1859, a sleeping car built for the purpose by 1865 and an eating and sleeping car

Liverpool & Manchester
Railway coach.

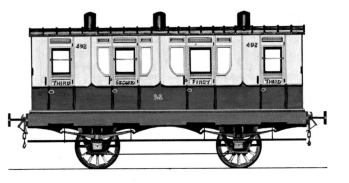

An early Great Western Railway coach and an open-topped third class coach as used on the Liverpool & Manchester.

by 1867 (for a Canadian railway). East and West were linked on 10 May 1869, when the Union Pacific and the Central Pacific Railroads met at Promontory, Utah, and a golden spike was driven to complete the rail connections in a ceremony in which the hammer blows were carried by telegraph across the width of the continent.

In Europe, British engineers, contractors and locomotives were prominent in the birth of steam railways. Robert Stephenson, for example, was active in Belgium (where his father was engineer to the first railway), in Denmark, Sweden, Switzerland, Egypt and elsewhere. Early Stephenson locomotives went even further afield, to Belgium, Germany, France, Russia, Austria and Italy, for example, as well as to the U.S.A. Thomas Brassey, using local labour spearheaded by a few of his trusty 'navvies' from Britain, managed contracts in many European countries, and also in South America, India, Australia and Canada.

The first Belgian railway, opened between Brussels and Malines in 1835, is notable as having been promoted, paid for and worked by the Government as part of a planned national system. The first German railway opened later the same year. A Canadian line between Laprairie and St John followed in 1836. All three railways had Stephenson locomotives. The St Étienne – Andrézieux Railway, the first in France, opened in 1828, but it did not carry passenger traffic until 1832. These railways were all later than one in the old Austrian Empire. It ran the eight miles from Budweis to Trojanov, and when it opened, with horse traction, on 7 September 1827, it was almost certainly the first in Europe.

The Dutch opened a line between Amsterdam and Haarlem and the Italians a line between Naples and Portici, in 1839. The Spanish decided in 1844 that they would use the five-foot six-inch gauge and opened their first line, between Barcelona and Mataró, to this gauge in 1848. Russia was early in the field, with the six-foot gauge Petersburg & Pavlovsk Railway opened from Pavlovsk to Tsarskoye Selo in 1836 and the 400-mile, almost straight St Petersburg–Moscow railway begun on the five-foot gauge in 1843 and opened throughout in 1851. Switzerland and Denmark, with first lines in 1847, were late on the railway scene, with Norway (1854) and Sweden (1856) still later.

Under British influence, an Indian railway was opened between Bombay and Thana in 1853, (5 foot 6 inch gauge) and the first Australian railway to carry passengers and goods opened with horse traction in South Australia in May 1854, followed by a steam line, between Flinders Street and Port Melbourne, in Victoria. There were nearly 128,000 miles of railway for public use in the world by 1870.

Quite apart from the obvious advantages of the railway in providing quick and cheap passenger travel and freeing industry from the need to be sited either near its main market or its source of raw materials, there were incidental benefits. For example, news spread quickly with the swift carriage of newspapers. Mails were speeded up, the Post Office being quick to take advantage of the new form of transport. The electric telegraph, the first reliable method of sending instantaneous messages, grew alongside the railway and was used largely for railway purposes. Railway timetables demanded uniform timekeeping instead of local time, so railway, and afterwards all other clocks, were synchronized on Greenwich time. As men travelled they took their thoughts, their ideas, their manner of speech with them.

Another effect was that the more wealthy were able to live further from their work, causing a movement away from better class houses in the inner ring of cities to the suburbs. The houses were often taken over, as time went on, by larger poorer families – or several families – and the rows of fashionable houses slowly degenerated to slums as the benefits of cheap travel moved down the social scale.

The effect on cities was multiplied by the growth of urban, as distinct from suburban, railways. It is perhaps a sober thought that the Metropolitan and Metropolitan District railways were hard at work in London before the first tracks met across the vast expanses of the U.S.A.

Telegraph Cottage,
Slough, on the Great
Western Railway, 1844

The Railway Age

As far as Great Britain is concerned, there is no real doubt that the Railway Age began with the opening of the Liverpool & Manchester in 1830, but for the world as a whole 1870 might be a better date to choose. By then, there were about 13,500 miles of railway in Great Britain.

In 1870 the British railway map was not unlike that of today, but there were great strides to be made elsewhere. The first pair of rails already stretched right across America, but only a fifth of the eventual network of lines existed. There was not a railway in China or Japan, or in most of Africa except the far north and far south. Great railway networks such as those of Argentina, Brazil, and Mexico, and smaller ones – Chile, Paraguay, Peru, and Uruguay – in South and Central America, were just taking their first tentative steps towards expansion. Four Australian states were in the railway age, the others were not, but New Zealand had a toe, though no more than that, in the doorway. Most of Europe was not far behind Britain, and Canada's 2,000 miles of track was only a twentieth of her eventual limit.

While the late-comers were building or developing railways on foundations already well laid elsewhere, the main stream of progress was leading to faster, more comfortable trains for passengers and better service for freight. Steam was still king and was to reign for many more years, but it was not long before, in 1879, a miniature four-wheeled electric locomotive built by Werner von Siemens was seen hauling up to thirty people at a time round a narrow-gauge track in the

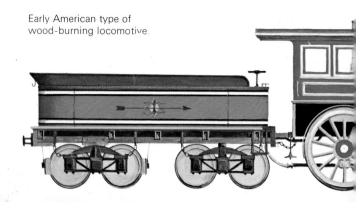

Early American type of
wood-burning locomotive.

Chicago & Atlantic Railway station in the early days when two Pullman car trains a day ran between Chicago and New York.

grounds of the Berlin Trades Exhibition. Though so small that the driver straddled it as though it were a horse, it was the first practicable electric locomotive and picked up its power from the track just as electric trains do today. Only four years later, on 3 August 1883, Britain's first electric railway opened. This line, which still exists, ran along the Brighton front and was

named 'Volk's Electric Railway' after Magnus Volk, then Electrical Engineer to the Brighton Corporation, who promoted it as a private venture.

Meanwhile, steam was showing what it could do, and there is no better example of the way improvements in speed were made than the London–Edinburgh 'Race to the North' of 1888. This arose from rivalry between the London & North Western Railway and its partner of the West Coast Route, the Caledonian, and the Great Northern, North Eastern, and North British Railways of the East Coast. In 1885 the West Coast trains took ten hours from London (Euston), and the East Coast from London (King's Cross) took nine hours for the 10 a.m. *Flying Scotsman*. This carried first and second class passengers only, but a train leaving London ten minutes later with first, second and third class coaches took only ten hours. The race really began when, in November 1887, the East Coast route started to carry third class passengers on the nine-hour *Flying Scotsman*. The West Coast Route soon became aware of a loss of passengers.

First the West Coast route equalled the nine-hour timing, then the East Coast made the run in $8\frac{1}{2}$ hours. West Coast plans to equal this were kept secret until the last minute, but on the

Werner von Siemens' successful 3-h.p. electric locomotive of 1879, which hauled visitors to a Berlin exhibition round a 900-foot track.

first day of the $8\frac{1}{2}$ hour service from Euston the East Coast came down to eight hours. This was on 1 August, but on 6 August the West Coast time was also changed to eight hours. So it went on with almost daily shorter times until a few days later the companies agreed that the East Coast route should take $7\frac{3}{4}$ hours and the West Coast eight hours. This rivalry, followed by newspapers all over the world, was the spur which brought out the best in railway men and equipment, and showed what could be done in the way of high-speed running.

All the trains involved in these races made a stop for lunch. At Preston, for example, passengers were expected to devour soup, a meat course, a sweet, cheese and biscuits, and coffee and be back in their seats in twenty minutes. It cost three shillings. But not all trains of the period stopped for meals. Already in 1867 the Great Western Railway of Canada had brought in a regular dining car service, using a car built by George Mortimer Pullman. In Britain, sleeping cars were introduced on the East Coast route in July and on the West Coast route in October 1873. American-style Pullman cars appeared on the Midland Railway in 1874: they had buffet bars for refreshments.

Speed rivalries in later years have also led to better public

Magnus Volk's electric railway at Brighton, the first in Britain.

service as, for example, the competition between the Pennsylvania Railroad, with its 902-mile, steeply graded route from New York to Washington and the New York Central, with its 'Water Level' route, much flatter but some fifty-six miles longer. The New York Central's *Twentieth Century Limited* and the Pennsylvania's *Broadway Limited* raced on these routes for many years, especially in the 1930s. In 1935, both trains ran the trip in seventeen hours, but already the writing was on the wall for steam. The pioneer streamlined diesel train, the four-car *Pioneer Zephyr*, had, in 1934, set up an average speed of 77·6 m.p.h. for the 1,015 mile run from Denver, Colorado, to Chicago, and diesel unit trains and locomotives were soon to oust steam, despite efforts to streamline steam locomotives and give them a new look.

In Europe the great international trains were largely in the hands of the Compagnie Internationale des Wagons-Lits, formed in 1876. The company provided luxurious cars for trains which covered, at quite high speeds, very long distances. Stops for frontier formalities made very high speeds out of the

A Stirling 'single' on the East Coast Route to Scotland.

question. The *Orient Express*, the first of these famous trains, began running in 1883 between Paris, Vienna and Istanbul and soon afterwards the company added 'et des Grands Express Européens' to its title. The second train was the 'Calais–Nice–Rome Express'. Then came Ostend–Vienna (1894), Paris–St Petersburg (1895) and a host of others. The company still operates today and its fine sleeping and dining cars – among the best in the world – can be seen on any trip to Europe. Its cars also offer Pullman-type services on many ordinary trains.

The railways themselves were still expanding. A start was made on the Pacific coast in 1891 on a railway which, at 4,607 miles, was to become the world's longest. This, the Trans-Siberian Railway, was opened as a through route in 1900, though this then included a considerable journey – about 1,400 miles – by steamer. In 1901 Wagons-Lits cars formed the 'Trans-Siberian Express' from Moscow as far as Irkutsk. The line, now greatly improved, is truly the backbone of the present Russian railway system.

Early scene on South Africa's three-foot
six-inch gauge railways.

In Africa, Cecil Rhodes dreamed of a railway route which
would link Cairo in Egypt with Cape Town and pass through all
the British possessions in the continent on the way. No through
line exists even now, though the trip is possible with some
railway steamer trips and a short road journey or two. Air
travel has made the through line unnecessary, but the railways
on the route were largely responsible for developing the
territories they serve. Egypt's first railway – a Robert Stephenson line from Alexandria to Cairo – opened in 1856 and South
Africa's first in 1860. Zimbabwe's first line, from the junction
with South African lines at the border to Mafeking, opened in
1894. By 1906 the rails had reached Broken Hill, 2,017 miles
from Cape Town. From here the route can be traced through the
Congo, East Africa, and the Sudan to Egypt, but there are
differences of gauge as well as gaps between railheads.

In 1910 the railways crossed the Andes. The Trans-Andean
line, between Chile and Argentina, reaches 10,515 feet in the
international tunnel through the ridge of the mountains. This

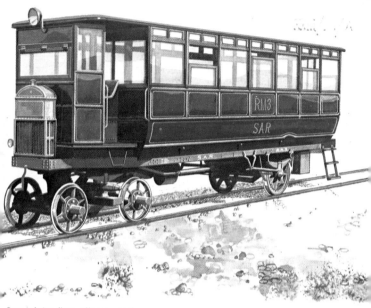

One of the first railcars used on
South African branch lines.

railway also suffers from having a different gauge from the
majority of the lines in the two countries it links.

Nowhere is the gauge problem more difficult than in
Australia, where the separate states originally all went their
own way. The Trans-Australian railway, however, was built
by the Commonwealth Government to connect the rail system
of South Australia with that of Western Australia, formerly
completely isolated. It was built to the standard gauge
(different from both the systems it links) and its 1,050 miles
include some 800 through waterless country. It runs 330 miles
in a straight line over the Nullarbor Plain. Now Australia is
tackling its gauge problem vigorously and providing new
standard-gauge connections.

Wherever the railways went, travel and trade followed and
grew. Sometimes they opened up remote territory, sometimes
they traversed country already well served by roads and
canals. In the early days in Britain the stage coaches tried hard
to compete with the new railways and in the late 1830s, at their

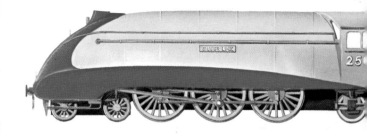

peak, they gave a remarkably efficient service. The growing speed of the railways beat them and their era of prosperity ended – quite quickly – as the railway trunk lines opened in turn. The canals lasted longer, because an efficient canal had and still has some advantages for heavy traffic when time is not important, but for most goods railway carriage soon proved more efficient, especially where the narrow canals were concerned.

War usually results in the running down of railways in the combatant countries – from wear and lack of maintenance as much as or more than through enemy action. Where they are really badly damaged, as in France in 1939–45, it can be a spur to postwar rebuilding with the latest equipment and result in a much improved system.

Apart from their role in carrying vital war materials in addition to their normal loads, railways can actually be instruments of military strategy. Light, narrow-gauge railways have been hastily built to carry troops and their supplies almost into the front line. A railway is almost essential as the supply route for an army in action, for nothing else can carry the load for long. The first railway laid specially for army support was that from Balaklava to the front line near Sebastopol in 1855.

It was the American Civil War which proved the importance of railways. They kept the armies of the North, far from their bases, supplied with food, weapons and ammunition. General Sherman's famous march through Georgia 'from Atlanta to the sea' was made possible by the railway stretching out behind him. It served the troops just as the Desert Railway stretching out from Egypt along the northern coast of Africa supplied the British Eighth Army in the last war.

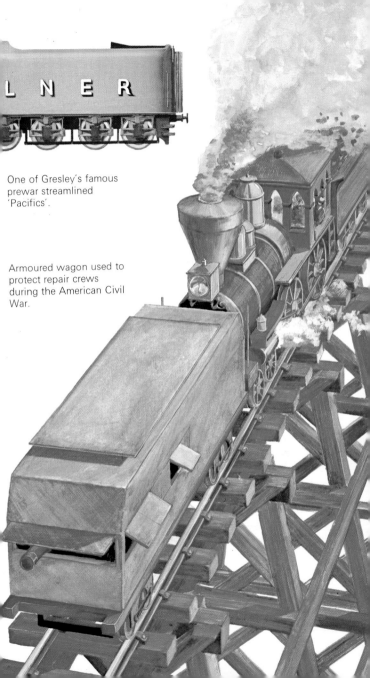

One of Gresley's famous
prewar streamlined
'Pacifics'.

Armoured wagon used to
protect repair crews
during the American Civil
War.

Trains for People

Railways everywhere are engaged in a war – a grim economic war – and in no field is it fiercer than in the battle for passengers. When the railways came they generated a demand for travel. The man who might never have moved out of his native district could now afford to travel fifty, a hundred miles, and the speed of railways gave him time to do it. Now the motor car has brought an even bigger boom in personal travel, and the railways, in their turn, are fighting a rearguard action in the same way as the stage coaches and canals did in the last century.

The car owner does not think about the cost of his vehicle, the depreciation, maintenance, insurance, taxation and the other payments involved in owning it. When he wants to travel he considers only the cost of his petrol – the other sums have to be paid whether he uses his car or not – and naturally he regards the car as cheaper than any form of public transport, especially if he has his family with him, and much more convenient because it will take him and his luggage from door to door. Motor cycle and scooter owners think the same. Are the railways, then, to be left with those too young, too old, or too poor to have their own transport?

In some places, notably the U.S.A., some railways have already reached the stage of dropping passenger transport altogether, but there is a special reason for this. Where distances are long, the speed of air travel is such that people will fly rather than undertake a long, comparatively slow drive. Although a train journey would relieve them of fatigue, the speed is still far less than that of an aircraft. So the railway is beset on all sides – by the car for short journeys and the aircraft for long.

Fortunately for railways there is a middle distance at which they are beginning to show they can excel. If speed can be raised enough, the advantage over the car becomes sufficient for business travellers – but not whole families travelling for pleasure. The convenience of the car is still attractive enough for the car to be preferred for journeys up to, perhaps, 100 miles. The exact figure depends on the frequency and speed of the train service and the type of road available, but 100 miles is a good round figure. Similarly, the inconvenient situation of most big city airports, involving perhaps an hour's journey by road at each end of the flight, reduces the speed advantage of aircraft over journeys of, say, 300 miles – again a very round figure. Somewhere in this middle zone lie hosts of journeys for which the railways have the chance to win traffic. They are seizing that chance with both hands.

In Europe, where many journeys between big commercial cities are of suitable length, train travel is still very popular – even booming. In the U.S.A., where distances are greater, passenger traffic is still in a poor way.

The need for speed is recognized: so also is the need for comfort. Passengers in all classes can expect comfortable seats, refreshment provision of one kind or another according to the length of journey, corridor coaches with washing and toilet facilities. On the more important trains they can expect –

Electrically-hauled train on the London-Liverpool-Manchester route.

sometimes at a slightly higher fare – to travel in luxury. Such trains are the Trans-Europ Expresses, a series of fast business trains linking 100 or so important commercial cities of Europe and running at speeds which equal or beat air travel for city-centre to city-centre journeys.

At first these trains were luxurious railcar sets powered by diesel engines so that there would be no difficulties from different forms of electrification in different countries, but now engineers can build electric trains able to run on three or four different systems and many of the new trains are electrically powered. The cars are soundproofed, first class only, often air conditioned, and have compartments for Customs staff so that the trains need not stop at borders. Originally all the trains were international, but later a few other trains built and operated to the same high standards – like the French *Mistral* – were allowed to use the title.

A German Railway Trans-Europ
multiple-unit diesel express.

All passengers are guaranteed a seat on these trains. A reservation system linked throughout Europe ensures that no ticket is sold unless a seat is available. The timetables are carefully arranged to suit the business man, being designed on the principle that he should be able to travel, have time to transact business at his destination, and return home on the same day. Here, in fact, was a service which started out by considering first what the customer needed instead of what was convenient for the railway to work. The reward has been spectacular success.

Many other business trains in Europe are timed with the need for out-and-home one-day trips in mind. For example, leaving Paris after breakfast, the business man can be in Strasbourg, 313 miles away, for a working lunch. Leaving Strasbourg before dinner, he can be in Paris four hours later. Many business trains have telephones through which the

The German *Rheinpfeil* electrically-hauled express with observation dome.

French electric locomotive for Paris-Amsterdam expresses.

Impression of an electric train for the New York-Washington run.
Power is picked up from an overhead line (not shown).

traveller can contact office or home. Some have hairdressing
salons or secretaries who will deal with urgent business
correspondence in any of several languages.

The success of good high speed passenger services is nowhere more apparent than in Great Britain, where the many
electrified services that form a transport network throughout
the country, connecting North and South, East and West,
result in domestic airlines finding it difficult to compete. And
trains are getting even faster. Many railways have 125 m.p.h.
in mind as a suitable express speed, and much faster speeds are
envisaged for the high-speed networks now planned – and
even partially-built – for Europe. The French, for example,
have 200 m.p.h. turbine units already running on normal
track, though they will have to wait for the new, precision-
built tracks, essential for stability at high speeds, to display
their 200 m.p.h. potential.

In Japan high speeds are reached daily on the New Tokaido

line, a new railway specially built, with all the latest techniques, for fast running. This line is being extended to give a run of nearly 700 miles from Tokyo to Hakata. Top speeds on the Tokyo-Osaka section began at about 115 m.p.h., but 160 m.p.h. or more is the aim for this and other new lines which together will make up a national 'Shinkansen' high-speed network.

In the U.S.A., where rail passenger traffic was once considered lost for ever, there is a remarkable renaissance of interest in high-speed rail services. The main target, with help from government funds, is the heavily populated 'corridor' running southwards from Boston through New York and Philadelphia to Washington. The Pennsylvania's new high-speed electric trains were designed to reach 110 m.p.h. in regular service and cover the 228 miles between New York and Washington in three hours. They have reached 156 m.p.h. in trials. These trains run on tracks already heavily used by ordinary trains. The U.S.A. is also experimenting with fast turbine-powered trains, and Canada recently built similar trains for regular service on the 338-mile Montreal–Toronto run, covered in about four hours. Russia also looks forward to 125 m.p.h. trains in the near future.

New Tokaido Line express at speed in open country.

Double-deck train for commuter traffic in the suburbs of Chicago.

High speeds are possible but expensive. The top speeds achieved with steam on the East and West Coast routes to Scotland before the war were possible only where there was a clear run with other trains kept out of the way for as much as twenty minutes ahead. This safety margin, necessary because the brakes and signalling of the day were not good enough to cope with 100-120 m.p.h. speeds, delayed other trains and therefore cost money.

Today signalling, brakes and track – for the wear on rails rises rapidly with higher speeds – are all being improved at the same time as the motive power; and this too costs money. But modern market research shows that travellers value speed very highly. British Railways, in fact, say that an increase in speed of 1 m.p.h. on a journey will result in an increase of at least one per cent in traffic. The railways are left to juggle the costs with the potential profits.

Another point is that fast and (relatively) slow trains cannot be mixed on the same tracks. With 120 m.p.h. passenger trains, 60 m.p.h. freight trains will have to be relegated to the night hours. One only has to draw the simplest of track space/time graphs to see the inordinate amount of track-time occupied by one half-speed train. The alternative is to have one route for passenger trains and another for freight – a solution possible only where a country is over-endowed with railways, as is, or was, Great Britain as a result of the competition of the earlier years. There is still the cost of maintaining two routes instead of one. Perhaps the real solution – a long term one – is to bring freight trains up to passenger standards. It would certainly cost a lot more for locomotives or other motive power and for rolling stock, but this could show a saving over the years if by ordering and using this advanced equipment it was possible to close down a complete route. Then passenger and freight trains would use the same track, the same signalling, and so on, increasing the volume of use to a point where the equipment could be employed to optimum advantage.

But not all travellers want to cover long distances at high speeds. Many want to travel quite short distances – say five to thirty miles – every working day at the right time to get them from home to their place of work or vice versa. No better way of handling large numbers of people in a short space of time and at a good speed has ever been invented. Into and out of Liverpool Street station in London flow up to 100,000 people

Electric multiple-unit coach for suburban services.

41

Travelling post office, with net for picking up mailbags hanging at the trackside.

in every peak traffic hour, and the story is repeated at other London stations and in great cities all over the world. The longer-distance 'commuter', as these regular peak hour travellers are known, expects, and usually gets, a comfortable seat and perhaps breakfast or bar facilities. For medium distances he expects a seat, if nothing else, and much ingenuity has been exercised in designing trains with the greatest number of seats in the space available. In many countries where the height of bridges, etc., permits, double-deck trains are used. On very short journeys on suburban routes and on underground or 'rapid transit' urban railways, the proportion of seats is small and most commuters stand in peak hours – though the seating is sufficient for the relatively small off-peak traffic.

It is the difference between the demands of traffic in and out of the peaks which makes commuter traffic such a headache for railways. Many trains are needed only for an hour or two in the morning and the same in the evening. Two sets of train men are needed to cope with two peaks – and the same applies to station and depot staffs, signalmen and so on – they must be at peak efficiency twice a day. Also, more tracks, better signalling, more equipment in general, are needed to handle the twice-a-day peak than would be needed if the traffic

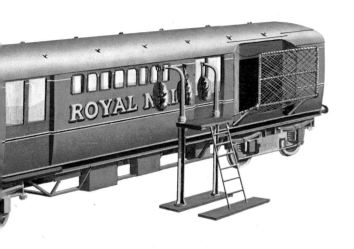

could be more evenly spread over a longer period of time.

To get the utmost use out of them, suburban trains are generally of the 'multiple-unit' type with the motors spread out along the train and a driving cab at each end. At the terminus, the driver moves to the other end of the train. The time saved in not having to shunt a locomotive from one end to the other is such that in some countries locomotives pull the train in one direction and push it in the other, the driver occupying a specially-fitted control compartment built into the end coach.

Passenger trains also carry some high-priority 'goods' traffic – notably newspapers, mails, and parcels. The mails were early railway passengers – they were carried on the Liverpool & Manchester from November 1830 – and they have been closely associated with rail travel ever since. One of the most spectacular aspects of this association is the travelling post office, a special van attached to fast trains for the purpose of carrying mail and sorting it en route: the first such van appeared as early as 1838. They are often equipped with apparatus which enables bags of sorted mail to be dropped at special wayside points while the train is travelling at speed. At the same time other bags can be picked up for sorting on the train during the journey.

Trains for Freight

With freight, we come to the reason for the very existence of railways. We have seen how the earliest railways were built to carry material won from the mines and minerals, and how this material and other heavy freight were the mainspring of railway building in many countries. Freight, rather than passenger traffic, is still the most important reason for the existence of railways, able to haul at considerable speed across country a load equivalent to the cargo of a fair-sized ship, and to do it with a crew sometimes as small as two and never more than a handful.

To gain the full advantages of railways, the load must be at least in the hundreds of tons and be carried considerable distances. Road transport can handle small consignments to many addresses as well as if not better than rail, and probably more quickly. Where the size of the consignments rises into

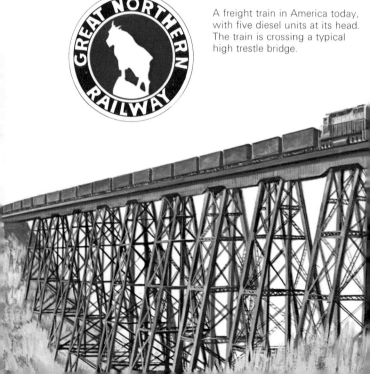

A freight train in America today, with five diesel units at its head. The train is crossing a typical high trestle bridge.

several tons, however, the railways have evolved effective means of handling goods which are proving highly competitive.

The most useful method of door-to-door transport used by the railways is the 'container'. Basically, this is a box in which consignors can pack all their goods themselves. The box is then carried by road to a railhead where it is put on a train for the trunk part of its journey. At the end of its rail trip it is put on another lorry for delivery. This system has been in use on British Railways for something like forty years, but it is only quite recently that the merits of the system have been universally recognized and the method widely adopted elsewhere. As well as special railway vehicles, there are ships and even aircraft adapted specially for container carrying. The great advantage to the customers is that the goods themselves are never handled or disturbed from door to door. For the railway, there are advantages in having only one large unit to handle. Containers can be of many sizes and types. Examples are

Piggy-back in the U.S.A.: road
trailers on flat wagons.

refrigerated containers for meat; containers with special
internal fittings to carry glassware, pottery, bicycles, etc.;
open containers for bricks, roofing tiles, etc.; and pressurized
containers for powdered materials which can be packed into
them or emptied by compressed air.

Sizes are now beginning to be standardized, although many
small, sometimes wheeled or collapsible (for returned empty
purposes), containers are not covered in this way. The larger
containers have an international standard of 8ft × 8ft by 10,
20, 27, 30 and even 40ft in length. Such containers can be
handled by standard cranes and other equipment and can be

packed on to lorries or wagons – or ships – as unit loads, the number per vehicle depending on the size. The name 'Transcontainers' is beginning to be used for these containers for international traffic.

A rather similar idea has an important application in North America, where the loading gauge allows vehicles to be raised higher than in Europe. Here the 'container' is a complete semi-trailer vehicle which forms the rear section of an articulated road lorry. The tractor unit is uncoupled and the complete trailer is loaded on to the train. At the other end of the (often very long) trip it is unloaded, another tractor unit is coupled to it and off it goes to the final destination. This has come to be known, for obvious reasons, as 'piggy-back' traffic. There are variations of the idea in Europe, the French having produced a particularly successful system in which the trailer wheels are run into special 'pouches' sunk below the floor of the wagon, thus reducing the height of the load. Again for obvious reasons, this has been named the 'Kangarou' system.

In some countries with gauge problems there is a further variant in that railway wagons of one gauge can be mounted on other, special, rail-fitted wagons of a different gauge to cover part of their journey and obviate unloading and reloading their contents.

Another important new idea is that of bulk trains – trains usually with a fixed number of wagons, all of the same type, which only rarely have to be uncoupled. They can carry a fixed quantity of, say, coal, iron ore, steel, oil, cement, or china clay and their running is worked out to suit a particular

Merry-go-round non-stop coal train in Britain.

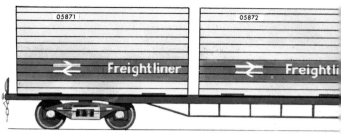

industry. They are especially useful where large quantities of raw or semi-processed material have to be transferred regularly from one point to another. A train may run several times a day or only once a week, but because it is known when and where it will run, what the load will be, how much engine power is needed, and so on, it is a very convenient unit for the railways to handle, and they can reduce their charges to firms offering such traffic. In Britain, there are many such trains for oil products and there are regular trains carrying nothing but motor cars on special wagons.

For bulk coal British Railways have come up with the 'merry-go-round' train. This is a train of large hopper wagons semi-permanently coupled together as a unit. They run from coalfields to bulk users, such as large power stations and, when they arrive, run slowly round a loop line without stopping. Apparatus on this loop line causes the bottom doors of the hopper wagons to open at the right places and the coal falls into hoppers underneath the rails. The bottom doors are also closed automatically and the train then runs back to the colliery, where it runs round another loop line. This time, as wagons reach the right spot, overhead hoppers load them with just the right amount of coal. British Railways have estimated that they could move, in these trains, five million tons a year in 205 wagons, instead of the 2,000 which would be needed for conventional working. The principle involved is of economising by getting good equipment and then using it intensively.

The unit train – a still more refined version of the bulk train – is obviously suitable for coal, ores, petroleum products (in tank wagons) and so on, but would not seem to be useful for

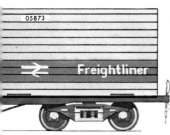

British Railways Freightliner high-speed flat wagon loaded with three standard containers.

goods in smaller quantities. With the container system, however, unit trains can also be used for these, provided there is a sufficiently regular flow of traffic between two points to make the service pay. This is the concept behind the Freightliner trains on which British Railways are placing great hopes. These trains take the container, not its contents, as the basic load, and the customer pays for the right to use the capacity of a container of one of several sizes. What he puts into the container is the customer's business. The trains consist entirely of specially-built high-speed flat wagons on which containers can be carried. There are special Freightliner terminals provided with giant straddle cranes which can transfer these containers from road to rail and vice versa very quickly and very gently.

Trackside apparatus reads number and ownership of moving wagon from coloured code.

The containers are distinctive in appearance and specially built of light alloy for the purpose. The initial routes are long ones where the high speed of these trains gives the greatest advantage – mostly between London and Scotland, but something like 100 routes and forty special depots may eventually emerge. The system has aroused great interest and many railways abroad have sent representatives to see it at work. A train of Freightliner wagons and containers of various types has toured Europe and a European Freightliner service is to be set up with the containers carried across the North Sea in specially-built ships. Harwich is being developed as a container-handling port and similar facilities are now in existence at Zeebrugge to form the European end of the ferry service. Other ports are also being fitted for container handling.

In the U.S.A. the Reading Railroad has decided that it will offer to send a locomotive, a brake van and a train crew anywhere on its tracks at any time, given two hours' notice, to haul a ready-loaded train of not more than 20 wagons direct to any other point on its system. This service gives the wagons a direct run without passing through marshalling yards, changing engines, or changing crews. In this way the railway can give at least as good a service as a whole fleet of lorries and often a better, faster one.

The special train has another advantage. In the past it was

sometimes held against railways that once a wagon had left a station no one knew where it was until it turned up at its destination. Goods sent by road, however, were in the personal care of a driver the whole time and if anything went wrong he would telephone his employer. This drawback, very real to traders under pressure from their waiting customers, is being tackled by the railways in a rather different way. Wagons are being fitted, at a standard height from the rails, with a special coded number plate which can be 'read' by electronic trackside apparatus. The apparatus can read all the numbers as the train goes by and transmit the information to a central point. By having a number of 'readers' the where-abouts of any wagon can soon be traced from the lists 'printed-out' automatically at the central office. Information from the readers can be flashed simultaneously to other points, such as the next wagon sorting yard ahead.

The idea of trains designed for one type of load only – minerals, steel, grain, cement, oil, cars, etc., – and even molten metal – has already been mentioned, but on some rail-ways such trains have grown to astonishing proportions. In West Africa, for example, many lines have been built solely to carry minerals and the trains on these railways may reach a huge size, because the cheapest way of working them is to run very few, very large ones. No matter what size, they need only one crew, and little signalling equipment is needed

Minerals in Mauretania:
trains of up to 17,000
tons run on this Sahara
ore railway.

because usually only one train at a time is on the main line. The LAMCO (Liberian-American-Swedish Mineral Co.) line in Liberia, for example, has 8,100 ton iron ore trains hauled by three diesel-electric locomotives and the 'Miferma' line in Mauretania is designed for 14,000 ton iron ore trains, also hauled by three locomotives controlled by a single crew.

As well as container-like trailer vehicles which can shed their road wheels for the rail portion of the journey, British and American railways have experimented with a container-like body fitted with both road and rail axles. These 'Roadrailers' have simple equipment, worked by compressed air, which can raise one axle and lower the other as required. The vehicles are light in weight and run as articulated trailers on roads. On rails, the front of each is supported on the one in front of it, the front car of all being supported by a special wagon with conventional railway coupling at the outer end. As railway cars, they can run at up to 70 m.p.h. and more. In Europe some countries use special road vehicles fitted with rails on which wagons can be carried through the streets to customers' premises.

Internationally, the scene is one of increasing the speed of

Carrying a railway tank wagon on a special road trailer.

freight trains everywhere. The United States has many trains running at an average of more than 50 m.p.h. over long distances. In Europe the picture is the same, helped by the Trans-Europ-Express-Marchandises – the equivalent of the passenger trains described in the previous chapter. This service, introduced to compete with fast road services on the motor roads of Europe, is still expanding, but already it has brought about some spectacular reductions in timings. Goods leaving Alicante in Spain early on a Monday morning can be in Dunkirk on Wednesday morning, having covered 1,270 miles, across frontiers, in fifty-six hours. In Europe, especially, freight traffic is speeded by the number of wagons owned by the various railways which can be used as their own by other railways. This 'common-user' pool of wagons is paralleled by similar pools of containers and pallets (platforms with or without sides, designed to be lifted by cranes or fork-lift trucks, on which goods can be loaded and firmly held, enabling the pallet load to be treated as a single unit). Container traffic in twelve major European countries is in the hands of an international railway-owned agency called Intercontainer.

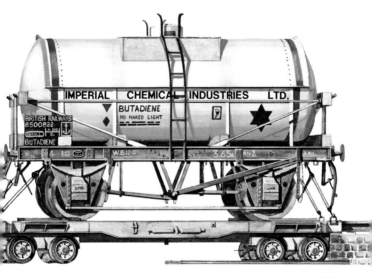

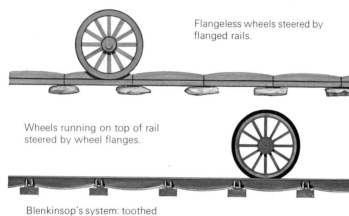

Flangeless wheels steered by flanged rails.

Wheels running on top of rail steered by wheel flanges.

Blenkinsop's system: toothed wheels, racks on outside rails.

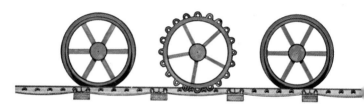

Tracks for Trains

The first requirement of a train is that it should have a track on which to run, and as far as railways are concerned the rails are as important as the vehicles which use them; they form the second half of the magic formula: steel wheels on steel rails.

Something of the earlier history of rail development was given in the first chapter. The first effective rails were of cast iron, like those of Jessop, but as soon as traffic on these rails became heavier it was found that cast iron was too brittle and wore too quickly, so the more expensive wrought iron was substituted. This in turn became inadequate and eventually, in 1857, the first steel rails were made by R. F. Mushet and laid at Derby in a location in which iron rails had worn out in three months. The steel rails lasted sixteen years. Steel gradually replaced iron everywhere, progress being accelerated by the patenting of the Bessemer process of steel-making in 1855 and the subsequent reduction in the price of steel.

Nowadays all rails are of steel. The rails by themselves could not support the weight of the trains and have to have a proper foundation to spread the load evenly over the subsoil.

The exact method of building the foundation differs according to the type of country in which it is built, the prevailing weather, the materials available locally, the weight of trains expected, and so on, just as roads differ in their composition. The track foundation not only has to spread the load, but has to be loose enough for the track to drain through it, to hold sleepers in place and level, and to give a certain springiness to the track.

The foundation materials, or 'ballast', are usually a broken stone such as granite or limestone, but can be slag, gravel, cinders, ash, sand, or even hard earth. There is usually a lower layer of large pieces of material, say three to nine inches across, and an upper layer of a half inch to two inches. On this the sleepers are laid and loose ballast of the smaller size is fitted in between them. The sleepers, or cross-ties, as they are more descriptively called in the U.S.A., are transverse pieces of wood or other material to which the rails are fastened. They hold the rails in place and at the right distance apart and also play their part in spreading the load. Sleepers may be of hardwood or softwood, of steel, of pre-stressed or post-stressed concrete, or of concrete blocks under each rail tied together by a metal bar. The choice of sleeper depends partly on local conditions, for there are some countries where timber sleepers

Modern high-speed track with
concrete sleepers and long welded rails.

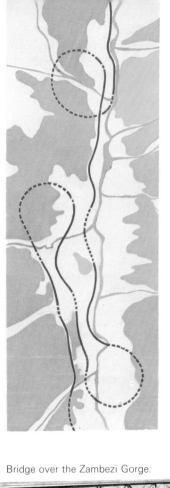

deteriorate rapidly or are attacked by termites. The number and spacing of the sleepers depends largely on the weight of trains, but in Britain there are some 2,100 per mile, in France 2,800, and in the U.S.A. from 3,000 to 3,500 on the most heavily loaded track.

A type of rail called 'bull-head' was much used in Britain. This has a rail section something like a dumb-bell, with a bulbous head on which the train runs, a thinner, web section below it and another, slightly less bulbous section acting as a foot. These rails

Spiral tunnels near Wassen on the St Gotthard line in Switzerland.

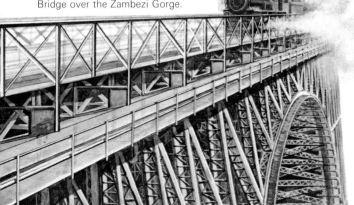

Bridge over the Zambezi Gorge.

are carried in cast iron 'chairs' shaped to fit them but with room outside the rail to drive in a wooden or spring metal block which holds the rail in place. The chairs are bolted to the sleepers or fastened down with coach screws.

Bullhead rails are still used, but most countries use a rail which has a bulbous head and a web section, but has a wide foot which can be spiked down direct on to the sleeper if needed, though generally some form of metal, rubber or plastics baseplate is inserted between rail and sleeper. These 'flat-bottom' rails are in use now on practically all high-speed tracks. The rails themselves have grown longer and are rarely less than sixty feet long. Most of those on main lines are longer – up to 100 feet or even more. The ends of the rails are joined by 'fishplates', short metal bars placed inside and outside the web of the ends of the rails with bolts passing through the fish-plates and rail ends.

Modern practice on fast lines is to weld the rail ends together to make rails of, say, 600 feet in length and then to weld them into even longer lengths after they have been laid. Such rails may be half-a-mile or even more in length but their elastic fastenings hold them without vibration or slipping under the passage of a train. To take care of expansion of the metal on hot days, the rail joints between lengths of long-welded rail are feathered, i.e. each rail is cut to a fine taper so that the ends can slide alongside each other without disrupting the running surface on which the train wheels run. Long welded track gives very smooth running without the constant beat of the rail joints so noticeable on other types of track.

Rails are laid with a slight inward slope, and the wheels of vehicles are coned to a similar shape when new. On a curve, therefore, as a train is forced outwards by centrifugal force the wheels move sideways so that the inner wheels are running on the smallest diameter and the outer wheels on the largest. This changing of wheel diameter helps to steer the train round curves and serves a similar purpose to the differential on a motor car.

A locomotive gives its best performance on the level and loses effect rapidly when it has to climb a gradient. The advantage of the steel wheel on steel rail is quickly lost. For this reason railways from the earliest days have been laid with gradients as small as possible. A good main line has few gradients of more than 1 in 200, i.e., a rise of one foot for every 200 feet of distance, though 1 in 100 is acceptable and steeper gradients are not uncommon. One steep gradient, however, can limit the size of trains over the whole line and make it necessary to use locomotives more powerful than would have been needed if it could have been avoided.

In hilly country obstacles cannot be avoided and the railway must make its own level path. From this need came the embankments and cuttings, the bridges, viaducts, and tunnels which form such prominent features of the railway landscape. Very steep ascents sometimes need exceptional measures, such as zig-zag lines on the side of a valley up which the train must be alternately pushed and pulled. In a few cases, trains gain

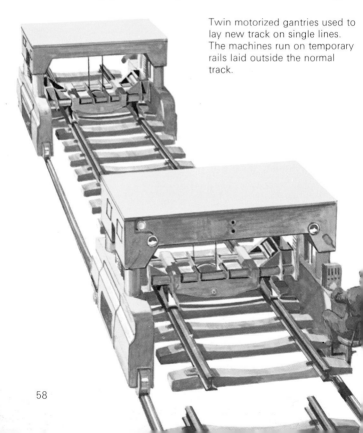

Twin motorized gantries used to lay new track on single lines. The machines run on temporary rails laid outside the normal track.

height by vanishing into a mountainside to appear again above, having executed a spiral turn in a tunnel. Railways can climb or descend via valleys in the same way, descending against the slope nearly to the bottom, crossing the river on a bridge and then turning to descend again with the valley slope. For still steeper inclines special methods, to be considered later in this book, are used.

Railway track is laid nowadays in complete panels, i.e. in lengths of rail to which the sleepers and baseplates, etc., are already attached. The panels are carried on flat wagons to the site and placed in position by cranes of many types, sometimes mounted on vehicles especially for tracklaying and sometimes rail or road travelling machines used for many purposes. Where longer, welded rails are to be used, the track is often

Keeping track in good order. This high-capacity tamper packs ballast under and round the sleepers and lines up the track automatically.

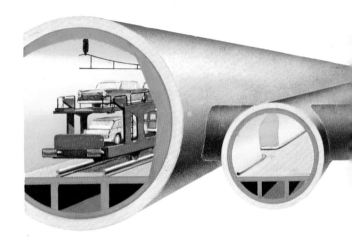

laid with short rails and left until it settles down under traffic. Then the short rails are taken out and the long rails fed over the end of a rail-carrying train into position on the track.

Track maintenance is now highly mechanized, with ingenious machines which can scoop ballast out, clean it, return it to the track, and push it under the sleepers to exactly the right height. The introduction of these machines has revolutionized maintenance work, and fewer men are needed. The men are now organized in large, highly mobile gangs with their own vehicles so that a large force can be used wherever required in conjunction with the machines. With modern apparatus, the work is performed much more quickly than before and the levelling and lining-up of the track can be performed automatically as the machines move along.

Railway tracks cross frontiers, as we have already seen, but they can also cross the seas. Railway wagons are carried across such stretches of water as the North Sea, the English Channel and the Baltic by train ferries with railway tracks on their main decks. There are ferries like them along the American Pacific Coast, across European and African lakes, and across wide rivers: they have been aptly named 'floating bridges'. Although the majority of these ships carry freight traffic, passenger coaches, with their occupants, are carried on others. For example, a sleeping car express, with the passengers in

How the Channel Tunnel might look, with electric trains in two main tunnels and a service tunnel.

A Swiss train ferry, the *Romanshorn* carrying passenger and freight vehicles across the Bodensee.

bed, crosses from Britain to the Continent regularly, and passenger trains are carried between Germany and Denmark.

Some wide rivers – like the Severn in Britain – are negotiated by tunnels, and now thought is being given to railway tunnels under the sea. A four-mile submerged tube has been laid across San Francisco Bay to take the tracks of a rapid transit railway. The Seikan Tunnel in Japan, fourteen miles of which is under the sea, connects the two main islands of Hokkaido and Honshu.

The long-proposed Channel Tunnel between Britain and France, so often on the brink of being started – and even begun in the 1870s and 1880s – will have at least twenty-one miles under water and be over thirty miles in total length. It will, with a fast electric train service, revolutionize rail communications between Britain and the Continent and be one of the most useful pieces of track ever built.

Railway tracks, like roads, are expensive to build and to maintain, so no railway has more of them than is essential. In these days of faster (but often fewer) trains and better signalling it is sometimes found that a railway has more tracks than it needs. It may be possible to reduce four tracks to three, with the third track signalled for two way traffic, or even to reduce down to two tracks. Similarly, one two-way track will sometimes perform the work which previously needed two one-way tracks. Good signalling and suitable passing loops are needed in these conditions and the best results are obtained where long stretches of track are under control from one point. Where trains are not too numerous, a hundred or more miles of line may be controlled from one centre. This centralized traffic control (C.T.C.) has revolutionized operations in parts of Africa, in North America, and now has a firm hold in Europe and the East. The principle is that from the central point the operator can see on a panel where every train is and the most convenient point for it to pass another train running in the opposite direction, and be able to operate, from a central panel, points and signals which may be controlled 100 miles away. Unless passing loops are very long, it is normally necessary for one of the trains to stop.

Points diverging from the straight can only be taken at low speed but new types of points, with very long tongues (the flexible sections of rail which move to contact the fixed rails on either side and thus change the direction of the train) enable the curves to be so smooth that the points can be taken at high speed in either direction.

Gentle curves are very important to high-speed train operation, which demands a high standard of track kept in very good condition. Any slight track defect scarcely noticeable in an ordinary train is magnified enormously in high-speed running. Heavy, well ballasted rails, properly laid and

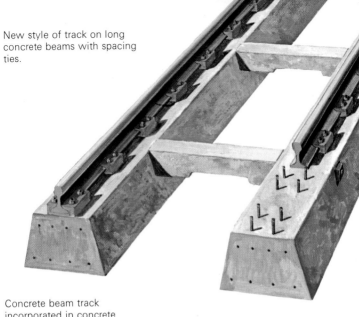

New style of track on long concrete beams with spacing ties.

Concrete beam track incorporated in concrete trackbase slab.

carefully maintained are now thought suitable for speeds of up to 185 m.p.h. or more, but sharp curves would have to be banked with the outer rail high above the inner. As an example, the high speed New Tokaido Line in Japan has curves with a *minimum* radius of 8,200 feet – more than $1\frac{1}{2}$ miles – and even this needs the outer rail to be nearly eight inches higher than the inner.

New methods of laying track are being tried out, including fastening the rails to longitudinal concrete beams under each rail or to concrete base slabs with various types of flexible pad in between rail and base, but so far the sleeper-mounted rail still seems superior to all others.

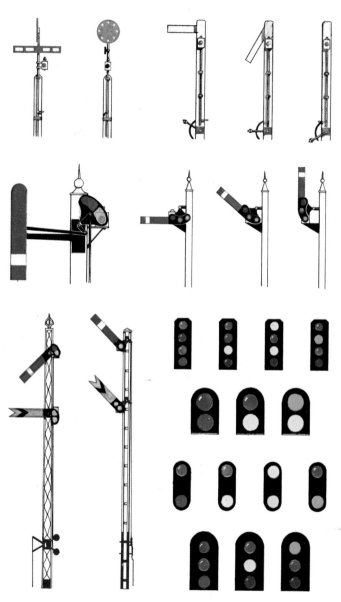

Train Safety

When railways were young signalling was not needed. With horses drawing a few trucks at walking pace there was no problem. Even with early steam, speeds were low and loads small, and often only one locomotive was running at a time. Signalling is still unnecessary on lines with only 'one engine in steam'.

As speeds rose the great advantage of railways – the low friction between rail and wheel – became a disadvantage because trains could not stop quickly, especially when only the locomotive and perhaps one or two manned vehicles had brakes. The 'brake van' was so-called simply because it was fitted with brakes which the guard could apply when the driver whistled for them. Once railway traffic grew past the point where trains were so few and far apart that they could never come together, something had to be done to tell drivers where other trains were.

From this need came the railway 'policemen', forerunners of the railway signalmen as well as of the police forces maintained by railways all over the world to keep order on their premises and guard against the pilfering of goods in transit. The Liverpool & Manchester had its police force from the earliest days, their police stations – according to the *Railway Companion* of 1833 – forming also 'depots for passengers and goods from or to any of the intervening places'. Hence the railway 'station'. To show drivers that the line was clear, the policeman assumed 'an erect position with his arm outstretched'. If the line was obstructed he stood 'at-ease'. Some railways also had signs for 'proceed with caution'. Unless the policeman had a long clear view down the line, the information presented to the driver usually depended on the length of time since the previous train had passed and therefore on the distance it could have been expected to run in that time. A red flag was used to stop the train to pick up passengers at the police station, so the

Top row: disc and crossbar signal (1840s) at danger and clear, and slotted semaphore at danger, caution, and clear. Middle row: 'somersault' semaphore at clear (1870s) and three-position 'upper quadrant' signal (1910 onwards) at danger, caution, and clear. Bottom group: a selection of modern semaphore and colour-light signals.

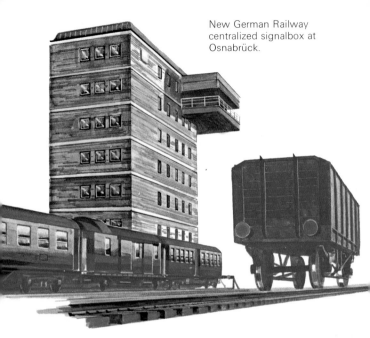

New German Railway centralized signalbox at Osnabrück.

red light came to mean 'stop' and trains carried a red tail light at night, though this was sometimes turned to blue when a train stopped as a special warning to the train following behind.

While the policeman had to show himself in person, he could attend to only one train at a time, so systems of fixed signals grew up which could be set and left while the policeman attended to another line. Flags or coloured boards were generally used by day and lamps by night, with varied colours.

Inside a centralized signalbox controlling many miles of track by signal and points switches mounted on its panel.

The London & North Western used white for 'line clear', green for 'caution', and red for 'stop'.

To give trains time to stop, signals were often displayed considerable distances before the danger points they protected. In this way the 'distance' – now 'distant' – signal came into being.

Flags sometimes hung down limply and could not be seen properly, so painted boards were often used, and the Liverpool & Manchester used a red-painted board which could be turned towards the driver for 'stop' but be in the edge-on position when the line was clear. Discs were sometimes used elsewhere. Boards and discs were often so large, for visibility, that holes had to be cut in them to reduce wind pressure. The railways were quick to see the possibilities of the early electric telegraph and experimental equipment by Cooke and Wheatstone was in use between Euston and Camden as early as 1837. As the telegraph came into regular use, railway lines were split into block sections and the passage of a train from block section to block section was telegraphed ahead from station to station. This system, still the basic method used by railways, is designed to ensure that only one train is allowed to be in a section at any one time.

Eventually, the idea of working signals from a central point by wires and levers came into being and the signals themselves crystallized into the familiar 'semaphore' arms, named originally after the Admiralty-type semaphore signalling chains in use at the time. The railway signals had an arm which signified 'stop' when horizontal and 'caution' when at an angle of 45°. To show 'clear' the arm slotted vertically out of sight into the post. This in turn gave way to arms which meant 'stop' when horizontal and 'clear' when at an angle either up or

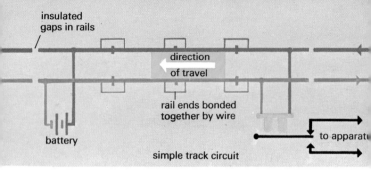

How a track circuit works.

A London Transport 'programme' machine which operates points and signals automatically from a punched timetable.

down. The 'caution' aspect was reserved for separate 'distant' signals with different coloured arms. At night, the lighting system evolved to green for 'clear', yellow for 'caution', and red for 'stop'. From these have sprung modern colour-light signals, visible by day and night for more than half-a-mile. (Over a mile for 'searchlight' type signals.) The busier sections of nearly all railways now have colour-light signals, but many semaphore signals are still in use. The modern section stretches from 'stop' signal to 'stop' signal (as opposed to 'distant' or cautioning signals) including a length of track beyond the signal. This is called the 'overlap'.

Modern signalboxes control all movement on the railway over a wide area instead of the mile or two dealt with by the older boxes at every station. All signalboxes have the same task, however, whether small or large – to ensure the safe working of all trains under their control and, after that, to ensure that they work in the quickest and best manner appropriate to the class of train. The older signalboxes have a row of big levers needing physical strength and skill to pull over. The levers are connected by wires or rodding to the signals and points and are all interlocked so that, for example, it is impossible to set the signals for one route and the points for another. As boxes grew larger and distances longer, power assistance was provided and the levers became smaller, until they were only a few inches long.

Modern signalboxes do not have levers at all, but small buttons, often geographically arranged on a diagram of the tracks they control, which have only to be pushed, pulled, or turned to change points or signals operated by electricity or compressed air miles away. Because points and signals often are out of sight of the signalbox, elaborate precautions are taken against the failure of the apparatus and detectors are fitted to signal back to the box that the required change has been made. This is shown to the signalman, usually, by a system of coloured lamps arranged geographically, like the operating switches, on a diagram. The movement of trains through the controlled area is shown on an illuminated diagram of the track. In later versions, the diagram is sometimes illuminated permanently *except* for the sections occupied by trains. This is a precaution against lamp failure.

The setting-up of a route through a complicated network of points and signals in a busy area can take some time, so a system has now been devised under which the signalman has only to push the two buttons at the beginning and end of the route for all points and signals to set themselves automatically. The apparatus is usually capable of 'storing' routes, so that the signalman can set more than one route in advance, the points and signals changing automatically to the next route as the first train clears the sections concerned. The signalman knows which train is coming next because, quite apart from the time-table, a code describing each train is passed from box to box – sometimes automatically – ahead of it.

On open track, where there are no junctions, trains can safely be left to signal themselves, each train turning the signal behind it to red as it enters the next section. When it reaches the section beyond, the red light, now two sections behind, turns yellow and the next, immediately behind the train, turns red. When the train then enters the next section, the first signal will turn green, so that every train leaves behind it, in order from the train, first a red, then a yellow, and finally a green signal.

All this is achieved, like the lights showing the train position, and nearly everything else in modern signalling, by track circuits. The simple track circuit is the foundation of modern signalling. The principle is that the track is divided into sections with insulation at the ends to separate them. A low voltage electric current is passed through one rail to the other end of the section and then back along the other rail. When a train enters the section it breaks the circuit and the current will take the shorter and easier path through its wheels and axles. The change in the track current flow is detected and many kinds of electrical apparatus can be controlled from this initial stage. When the train leaves a section, current flows through the rails again.

The London Underground has ingenious machines which carry the day's timetable, or 'programme' punched in code form on a plastic roll. As this roll passes through the machine it sets the points and signals correctly for the next train. When the train has passed the machine sets the track properly for the next one, and so on.

Signals may indicate the state of the track with the utmost reliability, but this is little use unless the locomotive crews can see them in all circumstances. To make their task easier, some railways now have apparatus which shows by colour lights in the cab the same indication as those shown by the normal signals. This is usually done by passing coded impulses through the rails, the frequency of the impulse indicating the state of the line and fixed signals and operating appropriately-coloured lights on the train – red, yellow, or green (double-yellow is sometimes used in colour-light signalling as an 'advance caution').

Cab signalling in Stockholm. Signals show as lights on the cab wall.

The extension of this system could well result in the disappearance of trackside signals altogether, for except in emergency they are not needed. On sections with signalling worked by the trains themselves, neither signalmen nor signals would be required.

The method of working long single lines by centralized traffic control (C.T.C.) has been mentioned before. It began in the U.S.A. in 1927 and can be as simple as the provision of a telephone at passing loops to let the train crews call in and report their position and ask whether they should wait for a train to pass or continue. Generally, however, there are power-operated points and signals at such loops with the controls concentrated at one or more desks at a central point. The

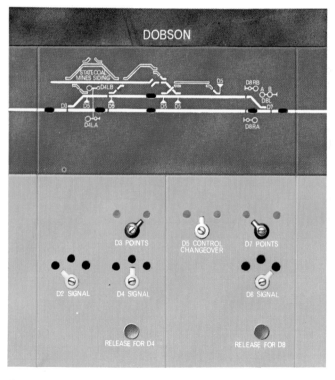

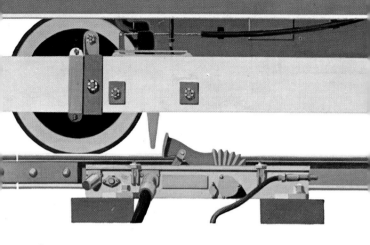

Part of a c.t.c. panel for control of points and signals (*left*).
A train stop on the London Underground (*above*).

controller at this point has a diagram showing him where every train is and can operate the whole stretch – possibly of two or three hundred miles – from his one desk. This saves manpower strung out along the line and also the many telephone conversations needed between spaced-out operators. The one man (or two) at the console desk can see the whole line and control it from one place.

Another safety device used on British Railways and elsewhere is the automatic warning system, which sounds a warning in the cab of a locomotive when a distant signal is passed at 'caution' or a colour-light signal at any colour except green. If the signal is at clear a bell rings, but if at 'caution' a horn sounds and the driver has three seconds to take full control. If he does not acknowledge the signal in that time by taking control the brakes are automatically applied. A visible indicator in the cab remains as a warning until the next signal is passed at clear.

Finally, some urban lines, including the London Underground, are fitted with a train-stop device at every 'stop' signal. If a train passes a signal at red a lever beside the track 'trips' a valve on the train and applies the brakes.

Tractive Power for Trains

The early development of the steam locomotive played an enormous part in the acceptance of railways as the dominant means of inland transport in the last century or more. Without it we might not have had our present national networks of railways at all. Steam was the leading source of power in the nineteenth century for all kinds of industrial activity – steamships, mills of every kind, factories, even for ploughing on the larger farms, and the steam railways fitted logically into the business of industrialization.

Over this long period the powers of the steam locomotive were developed by a race of engineer aristocrats to a point of which Stephenson can never have dreamed. They became fast – Britain holds the record with 126 m.p.h. by Sir Nigel Gresley's streamlined *Mallard* – and powerful – the U.S.A. had 570-ton locomotives capable of hauling 18,000 ton ore trains. A steam locomotive could be built for almost any task. Why then, though continuing to do fine work in many parts of the world, have they vanished from many areas, and are they on the way out in many others?

The reasons are both economic and social. The diesel and electric locomotives which are taking the place of steam are more costly than their predecessors, but they are available for work over much longer periods. A steam locomotive had to visit a depot for attention every day. When its fire was out it took a long time to light it and reheat the boiler and raise a working pressure of steam.

This higher availability makes the more expensive equip-

ment cheaper in the end. For example, a diesel shunter can work twenty-four hours a day for a whole week or more before paying a visit – a short visit – to its depot. Because the diesel or electric locomotives can do more work, fewer of them are needed. Further, they can usually maintain a higher average speed than steam units and can work more trains as a result. In fact, steam locomotives were never very efficient at turning coal into energy – only about seven per cent of the available heat was used – and the same coal could be better used in a power station to produce current to drive an electric locomotive. This situation was made worse by a world shortage of the large coal on which locomotives ran best – attributed to mechanical mining methods breaking the coal down more than hand mining. Oil firing has been adopted in some countries to overcome some of these difficulties.

Steam locomotives needed a driver and a fireman, but diesel and electric locomotives need only the driver, though it may be that there is a case for a second man on long distance trains. Socially, too, the necessarily dirty nature of steam locomotive work of all kinds, including maintenance as well as driving, has become unacceptable.

Electric and steam locomotives existed side by side for a long time, the cost of electrifying lines ensuring that electric trains were confined, generally, to the more important routes. The diesel locomotive, however, could run on the same tracks as the steam locomotive and also observe the same signals. The diesel challenge was more immediate and more urgent than anything which had gone before.

The first diesel locomotive ran in 1894 in Hull, with an

A Garratt-type locomotive with one boiler feeding two engines.

engine designed by W. D. Priestman, and another early designer was Akroyd Stuart, but it was not until Dr Rudolf Diesel saw the possibilities of the engine which now bears his name, and its railway potentialities, that the diesel locomotive began to assume importance. Very briefly it is a compression-ignition engine: oil fuel is ignited by the heat generated by the compression of air. Because air only is compressed, instead of a fuel-air mixture as in a petrol engine, there is no risk of a 'backfire' and the compression ratio can be much higher than with, say, a car engine.

The load on a locomotive is much higher than on a road vehicle, so the problem of transmitting the power of the engine to the wheels is more difficult. The engine must run at a fairly

A typical single-cab General Electric diesel-electric locomotive body.

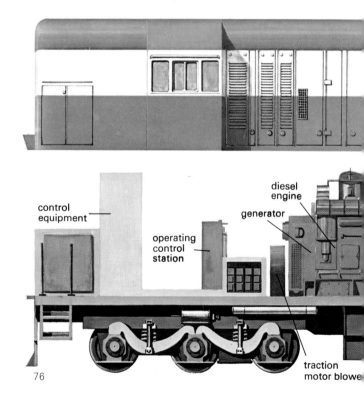

control equipment

operating control station

diesel engine

generator

traction motor blowe

76

high speed to develop full power; it cannot start on full load like a steam engine.

There are three main ways of transmitting the power. For small locomotives and railcars mechanical transmission can be used, much the same as in a lorry, with a gearbox to select the appropriate ratio between engine speed and road speed. The main difference is that some form of fluid flywheel or fluid coupling is nearly always used instead of a normal friction clutch, allowing the load to be taken up smoothly.

The main type of drive used on the world's diesel locomotives, however, is less direct but more flexible. The diesel engine has no connection with the wheels but drives a large generator. This in turn drives electric motors which turn the

How the main equipment of a diesel-electric locomotive is arranged (bottom). This versatile type is available for several gauges.

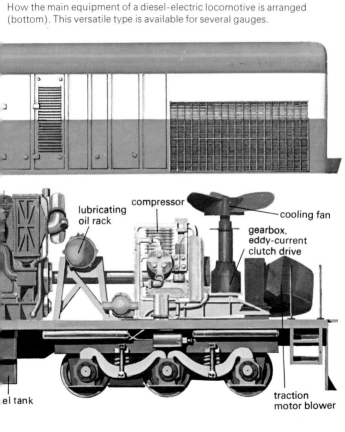

wheels through gearing. The principle is simple and the drive very effective. There is no gearbox to worry about since the electric motor, like the steam engine, adapts itself to the load.

There is another type known as the hydraulic drive, which has been developed mainly in Germany but has been adopted on a fairly wide scale elsewhere. The engine in this case drives a torque converter, which is a hydraulic means of magnifying or reducing the power put into the driven end to give more or less power, at lower or higher speeds, at the other end. The engine drives a type of centrifugal pump, called the 'impeller'. This forces the fluid filling the torque converter casing against the blades of a turbine, causing it to rotate and drive a shaft which, through other shafts and gearing, drives the wheels.

The 'straight' electric locomotive has been with us since

Right: the *Mistral* en route between Paris and Lyons. Below: head-on view of South African electric locomotive with *Blue Train* roundel. Bottom: Swiss electric 'push-pull' train running locomotive first.

1879, when Werner von Siemens's first tiny locomotive ran for four months hauling passengers at the Berlin Trades Exhibition, and there is little doubt that the railway future lies in electrification.

Electrification, however, is costly because it needs a whole system of electrical substations and cables to bring the power to the track, and the track itself must have, along its whole length, either an overhead supply (catenary) or an extra rail which the trains can continuously tap to pick up power. It can only be used, therefore, for lines carrying heavy traffic. For main line electrification the overhead system is carrying all before it, but for shorter, urban and suburban services, third, or third and fourth, rail systems have much to commend them. For underground railways they are almost essential, as they reduce the headroom needed and hence the cost of tunnelling. Power may be supplied as either direct or alternating current ('d.c.' or 'a.c.'). Until quite recently it was generally thought that d.c. motors were much the best for locomotives, and these are still the main type used. The current supplied from power stations is always a.c., which can be transmitted, at high voltage, at a reasonable cost. The first task of a substation is to lower this high voltage to one suitable for transmission over the railway network. If the railway uses third rail distribution the substation also has to 'rectify' the supply, turning it into

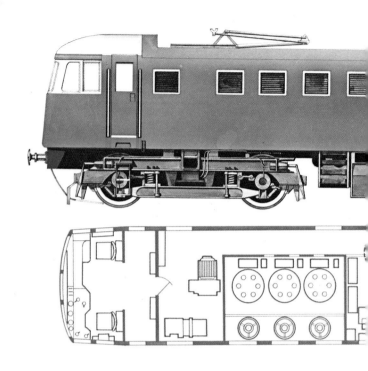

British Railways 3,300-h.p. a.c. electric locomotive. The three rectifiers which convert a.c. to d.c. are on the centre line to the left.

direct current at a comparatively low voltage. For example, the Southern Region of British Railways uses 750 V. d.c. for its third rail system. Other d.c. systems may use higher voltages, up to about 3,000, but with overhead distribution to the trains. The locomotives can either use this current at the voltage at which it is picked up or step it down before it is fed to the motors.

When alternating current is supplied, as it is in the latest systems, it is distributed by an overhead catenary at a high voltage, e.g. 25,000 V., and at the normal industrial frequency supplied by the power grid of the country concerned – in Britain, fifty cycles per second. This high voltage is first transformed to a lower voltage in the locomotive and then either

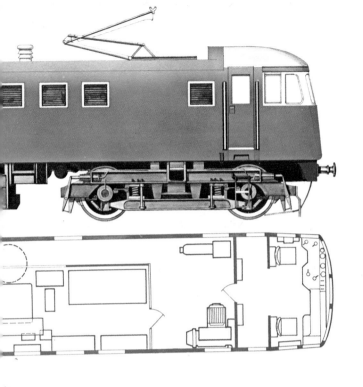

used to feed a.c. motors or rectified for d.c. motors. In the confined space of a locomotive it is essential that apparatus for rectification should be kept small, and great strides have been made with transistor type rectifiers using either silicon or germanium. The use of high-voltage a.c. enables much lighter overhead equipment to be used than is needed for lower-voltage d.c. and also fewer substations are required.

As with diesel-electric locomotives, the final drive in electric locomotives from motors to axles is through a gear train, and the ratio of these gears can be adapted to the work for which the locomotive is intended. Thus one unit could be geared for high speeds with light loads and another unit for heavy loads at low speed.

Electric and diesel-electric locomotives can make use of electrical braking, reducing the wear on the wheels caused by applying the normal brake blocks. In effect, the electric motors are switched to operate 'in reverse' as generators driven by the wheels. In generating current they absorb energy and brake the train. The electrical energy has to be dispersed as heat through banks of resistances (rheostatic braking), but straight electric locomotives can be arranged to feed the power back into the current supply system (regenerative braking).

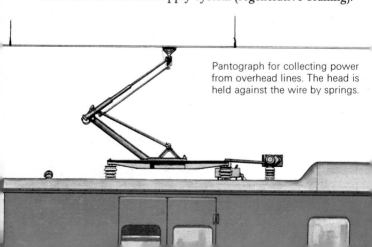

Pantograph for collecting power from overhead lines. The head is held against the wire by springs.

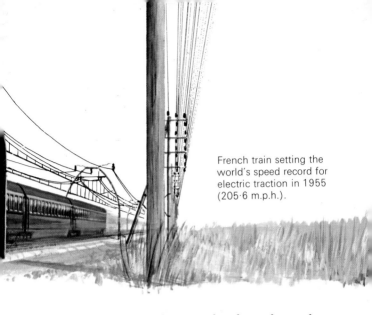

French train setting the world's speed record for electric traction in 1955 (205·6 m.p.h.).

In postwar years the French National Railways have taken the lead in experiments with industrial frequency electrification, and in tests made in 1954–55 they achieved some remarkable results with special test trains and suitably geared locomotives. Two locomotives, on successive days, hauled the streamlined three-coach test train at 205·6 m.p.h. Spectacular as this effort was, the more mundane tests undertaken to prove the reliability of electric traction were probably more important and far-reaching in persuading other countries to adopt similar electrification schemes. Perhaps the most important point is the enormous power reserve of electric locomotives, which, drawing on a central source instead of generating their own current, can give much more than their nominal power for short periods. This enables them to accelerate swiftly and to run at an even, high speed regardless of gradients. Electric locomotives can now be built to run on more than one type of current supply, simplifying the working of through trains over railways with different systems.

Diesel and electric locomotives can both be worked 'in multiple', which means that two or more locomotives can be coupled together and operated by a single crew. Some

American trains can be seen with five or six diesels at their head, all worked by one crew. As the pull of all these loco-motives tends to put a great strain on couplings – and some-times breaks them– the modern tendency is to put the extra locomotives at various points along the train, controlling them by a radio link from the locomotive at the head of the train. A later development is control by sensitive apparatus on the 'slave' locomotive which detects when the brakes are being applied or when more power is needed by the behaviour of the part of the train ahead.

Although we have dealt with locomotives so far, exactly the same types of motive power can be applied to multiple-unit trains, i.e. trains without locomotives but with small, often under-floor, power units distributed among the cars. The lighter diesel railcars usually have mechanical transmission, but the more powerful ones can have either electric or hydraulic transmission. Electrical controls allow gear chang-ing, etc., to be carried out simultaneously along the train in the same way as with locomotives running in multiple.

Freight trains are always locomotive hauled, though multiple-unit freight train sets have been mooted before now, but passenger trains can either be multiple-unit or locomotive hauled. Which method is used depends largely on whether a train is always to be of the same formation, irrespective of the number of passengers wanting to travel, or whether the addi-tion of extra vehicles at peak time is necessary. In the latter case, the locomotive is the answer, though it is sometimes possible to add an extra car (or luggage van) to a multiple-unit train designed for the purpose. Many people consider that a locomotive-hauled train gives a smoother, quieter ride and is preferable for longer distances. The power cars of some fixed-formation trains are as powerful as many locomotives and can be loaded accordingly, but generally the power of a multiple-unit train is no more than is needed for the service for which it was designed. To make it otherwise would be wasteful.

There *are* electric shunting locomotives in some countries such as Switzerland, but generally it is not economic to electrify a shunting yard on the overhead system and dangerous to do it by electrified rails when staff have to walk along to examine wagons and loads. For this reason, shunting

European type of diesel shunter with steps for staff.

is nearly always done by diesel locomotives – either diesel-mechanical for low powers or diesel-electric or diesel-hydraulic for higher ratings. They are usually geared to give a big hauling capacity (a high 'tractive effort') at low speeds, but some of the larger types are arranged to be able to work short trips if required with freight trains or even passenger trains when no heating is required.

Many experiments have been made with gas-turbine loco-motives, and quite a number are in use, but it has been found that such locomotives are not economical unless they can be used in conditions which keep them working at full power. In practice, this means long uninterrupted runs with heavy trains, and such conditions are found in few European countries. In the U.S.S.R. and America there is more scope, and the Union Pacific has some seventy gas-turbine locomotives, mostly 8,000 h.p. units used to haul heavy coal trains of up to

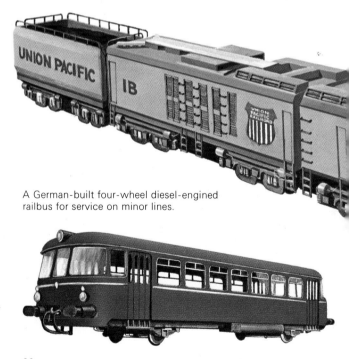

A German-built four-wheel diesel-engined railbus for service on minor lines.

5,000 tons on a 500-mile stretch of line with heavy gradients which rises to over 8,000 feet above sea level. This combination of long run, high altitude and heavy load is ideal and the gas-turbines do well here, but they have not been adopted on this scale elsewhere.

A new generation of small gas-turbines based on aircraft types is now appearing on experimental trains, however, and these give such high power for weight – 1,100 h.p. from a recent three-ton French unit, for example – that they may well have a considerable future. Both Canadian and U.S.A. railways have trains using these new units (which are compact enough to go under the floors if required) and the French reached 144 m.p.h. in July 1967, with a two-car unit powered by the 1,100 h.p. gas-turbine just mentioned. For high speed work these units could be ideal and are being developed.

As well as the multiple-unit trains we have discussed, there is a future in undeveloped countries and on branch lines else-where for light, self-powered diesel vehicles to carry passengers, mails, parcels, etc.

Powerful three-unit gas-turbine locomotive used on heavy coal trains by the Union Pacific Railroad.

Small country station with sufficient amenities for light traffic.

Handling Passengers

Journeys by railway begin and end at stations, and, small or large, they are the railway's shop window and must offer the passenger all he is reasonably likely to need in the way of service. In a country village this may be no more than a halting place alongside the track, without, in some countries, even a platform or shelter, as long as it is a recognized place for the train to pick up and set down passengers. A large city terminus or through station, on the other hand, must offer nearly every personal service a passenger could think of except perhaps a bed for the night – and many large stations have railway-controlled hotels attached to them. A well-equipped station, with its waiting rooms, refreshment and dining rooms, bath-rooms and hairdressers' saloons, has in fact been called a 'day hotel'.

The main purpose of a railway station, however, is to provide a place where all the functions required to get a passenger and his luggage into or out of railway trains can be performed as effectively and speedily as possible. The first need of the passenger is to know what trains are available to his destination, how long they take and where, if anywhere, he has to change. This information is all shown on printed timetables and train indicators in any fair-sized station, and if there are any other questions, such as whether a meal can be obtained on the train, there is an enquiry office to help the traveller. As well as answering questions, such offices can usually supply, free of charge, pamphlets giving train services on particular routes and free leaflets describing towns and cities of interest on the system.

On most services our traveller needs no more than his ticket, but if he is travelling by a popular train or wants a sleeping berth, he will have booked these, and his ticket, in advance. The 'booking' of a ticket dates back to the days when particulars of a traveller's journey really were entered in a

Large through station with many platforms and full passenger facilities. Steam locomotives have now vanished from British railways.

book, but nowadays he is given a pre-printed ticket or a ticket printed on the spot by a machine in the booking office. Such machines are often arranged to make an automatic record of the sale for accountancy purposes. Reserved seats are marked off on a train plan, and most larger stations in Europe and the U.S.A. can book seats on trains in many other cities, either by telephone or by computerized reservation services which keep a central record of all bookings at a large number of stations and can tell any station which seats – or sleeping berths – are available and on which part of the line.

For many luxury and businessmen's trains, tickets will not be sold unless seats are known to be available. In summer, when many people want to travel on holiday, especially at weekends, seat reservations increase in volume as people make sure of their comfort. Again, the number of tickets sold for particular trains sometimes has to be limited, especially where the trains connect with ships of fixed passenger capacity. Sometimes station staff have to be experts at crowd control,

Booking-office machine for printing tickets as required by passengers.

keeping waiting passengers in queues while their train arrives and is cleared for their journey.

Even holiday crowds are dwarfed by those carried for special sporting events. Although not so many in total number, such crowds want to arrive, and still more depart, all at the same time. Stations near sports stadiums are usually specially designed with extra capacity to allow thousands of people to flow smoothly into and out of trains which appear, one behind the other, with clockwork regularity. To see London Transport dealing with a Cup Final crowd at Wembley Park station is an education in mass movement.

Analogous to special services for sports are excursion trains to pleasure spots and special events, such as seaside or lakeside towns, air displays, athletic meetings and so on. Excursion

Passenger-operated ticket machine selling many kinds of Underground tickets.

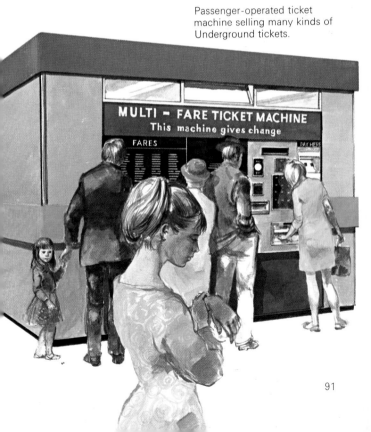

trains have a long history, and were already popular by 1840. Special cheap fares are offered for travel by that one train only and the routes used are in some cases never employed by ordinary trains. The longer-distance excursion train usually has a buffet counter for refreshments and is worked by coaches which would otherwise be idle – a factor which, together with the high percentage of seats usually taken, makes it possible to offer the low fares.

At most big city terminals there is a daily morning inrush of people who work in the town and a corresponding outrush at night as they go back to their homes in the suburbs. These 'rush' or 'peak' hours are difficult and expensive for railways to handle, for they use so many trains during the two peak periods that no work can be found for many of them during the rest of the day. (The same 'peak' problem occurs with summer holiday weekends, for which extra coaches must be available. Such vehicles may only be needed for half-a-dozen runs a year.) To meet the peaks, the railways have to tie up their capital in trains, extra platforms, extra tracks and apparatus, and extra staff, none of which would be needed if the traffic could be spread over a longer period by staggered hours of work for commuters.

With so many passengers travelling regularly, an army of booking clerks would be needed if everyone had to have a separate ticket for every journey. The familiar answer is the season ticket, lasting for a week, a month, three months, or longer, with the attraction of a reduction in the cost per day as the length of availability of the ticket goes up. This saves the railway clerical work and the passenger a great deal of time. Another method, familiar in London and in some other large cities, is to sell tickets of frequently-used values by machine. Such machines can be made to accept a variety of coins and give change as well as a properly-printed, valid ticket. Banks of machines can take care of the most frequently demanded tickets, leaving the booking clerks free to deal with the less common varieties.

Where there are mass movements of passengers, or 'commuters', as daily travellers are usually called today, great attention has to be paid to the design of stations to ensure that passengers can reach trains easily and disperse quickly,

Railway excursion poster for the
Great Exhibition of 1851.

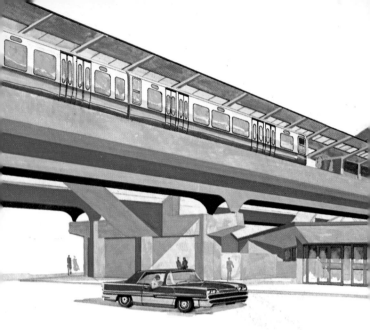

particularly the latter because passengers arrive to join trains either individually or in small groups but a train may deposit a thousand or more passengers on the platform within a few seconds. A free flow is essential, with enough ticket collectors and ticket gates to let people through without too much crowding in the gate area. Their tickets inspected, some commuters will walk away from the station, some will join buses, some private cars, and if there is an underground railway many will want to join that.

The last need is the most easily catered for, since with an efficient system of subways, stairways and escalators, arranged so that streams of people moving in conflicting directions are kept apart, the passengers will move themselves from one means of transport to the other. Bus lanes, or standing areas where the station is a bus terminal, should be reached under cover and by subway (or bridge) if there are roads to cross. Some suburban stations may have an official who co-ordinates bus operation with the arrival of train loads of people, despatching buses when full and calling up the next scheduled bus or an extra. (This method is frequently

A modern urban station with platforms on a viaduct and ticket office, etc., below. Bus passengers can transfer under cover.

used when special trains are arriving for sporting events.

Other passengers arrive at or leave stations by car. If they are driving themselves they need car parks where the car can be left in the morning and picked up in the evening. Where railways have enough land they are catering for this traffic as fast as car parks can be prepared. Not only does the passenger pay his fare but also a parking fee, so that the operation can help railways to pay their way. If no car park is provided the car-owner may decide to drive all the way to work and back and his custom is lost.

Other passengers are driven to the station by their wives who then drive home again and have the car for their own use all day. This is known descriptively in the U.S.A. as 'kiss-and-ride' traffic as opposed to the owner-driver's 'park-and-ride'. An essential is a waiting space near the station entrance where the wives can wait for their husbands in the evening and a through road where they can drop them off and drive away in the morning. This can usually be the same wide road. The same road can be used for the comparatively small number who arrive and depart by taxicab. At large city terminal stations parking space for private cars is often impossible to provide, so the proportion of people using taxicabs increases and space must be found for a cab rank.

Apart from passengers making internal journeys, there are many travelling from one country to another, and, traditionally, the railways have always been in the forefront in providing facilities. There is a long history of railway-owned ports and railway-owned vessels, on the short sea routes of Europe, the great lakes and rivers of Africa, and elsewhere. At such ports, the railways provide premises for passengers to go through customs and passport formalities, and the railway ships sometimes have a passport office and the officials of one or both countries on board. They also provide offices on board where currency can be exchanged, as well as duty-free shops and bars. The ships themselves are miniature liners with the latest navigational facilities, stabilized, fast, and capable of keeping the seas in almost any weather.

Some passenger ports now handle containers, too, like this one – Harwich.

A recent development is the serving of airports by the railway which provides an excellent transport system for the traveller. Airports that are situated close to railways are in an excellent position for a fast shuttle service to transport passengers to the terminal or a short spur line can be built – London's Gatwick is a good example.

As airports and aircraft grow in size, however, and as more people make use of the many internal flights now available, the picture is changing. Heathrow Airport's four terminals are now served by the Piccadilly Line and an extension of the rapid transit system in Cleveland is already serving the airport there. As traffic possibilities increase, the building of a railway becomes a more attractive proposition both commercially and socially, though paradoxically a swift service to and from a city airport could weaken the competitive value of mainline express trains compared with aircraft.

Where no other form of transport is involved and the trains themselves cross frontiers, it is sometimes necessary for passengers to alight on one side of the border and file through buildings where passports, etc., are checked by the officials of both countries, the train meanwhile crossing the frontier empty after examination by frontier officials. The train then waits on the other side for passengers to reboard. On many trains, however, the passengers stay in their seats while officials walk through the train, or the officials travel with the train and perform their work en route.

On international trips of this kind the traveller can avoid frequent inspection of luggage by 'registering' it at the station of departure. It then travels to the passenger's destination without his touching it again, but must be examined by customs officials where he alights. For internal journeys cases, etc., can also be handed over for carriage in the luggage van, but in these days when passengers travel light there is usually room either in the compartments or saloons, or on racks at the ends of the coaches, for luggage to travel with the passenger under his own care.

Some of the facilities provided for passengers were men-

Services are brought to passengers on
the platforms during stops.

Books

98

tioned at the beginning of this chapter, but railway catering must be put first. The variety is wide, ranging from excellent, reasonably priced meals in dining cars en route to packed meals bought on station platforms; from beautifully panelled bars on luxury trains to drinks trolleys pushed along corridors. In Europe, especially, the station restaurant is often one of the best in the town and the favourite eating place of many besides passengers.

Railways can provide surprising services, once the need is known, such as having hire or self-drive cars to meet trains – the self-drive cars can later be left at another station if required – or providing an invalid chair to wheel an infirm passenger from train to taxicab. Kiosks for confectionery, bookstalls, flower stalls, postal counters, banks of telephones, and telegraph offices are taken for granted at larger stations, as is the background music played on the public address system between announcements, but television screens to show how approaching trains are running are still rare enough to provoke comment among even hardened travellers. One day they will be everywhere. Stations will be – as some are now – much more than the starting point of a journey.

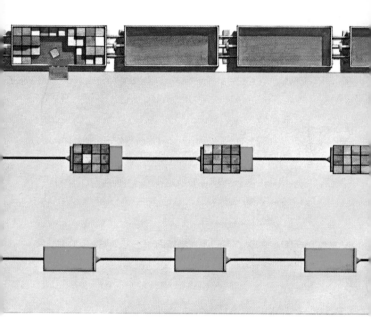

Handling Freight

Unlike the passenger, freight does not often present itself at a railway depot ready to be put on a train. It is more usual for it to be collected from the sender's premises by a railway-controlled vehicle, though sometimes the consignor will deliver it to the railway in his own vehicle. Bulk loads, such as coal or ore, usually start from a complex of privately-owned sidings owned by the colliery, mine, or dock and end their journey at a similar complex owned by generating station, processing plant, or whatever it may be. These traffics, therefore, are presented as wagon or train loads and need no special railway terminal facilities. All freight, however, has to begin and end its journey at a terminal of some kind and these have to be carefully designed for the type of traffic they are expected to handle.

A small consignment of freight arriving at a railway freight terminal will normally already have been documented on or before collection. If not, this is done when it arrives. In some

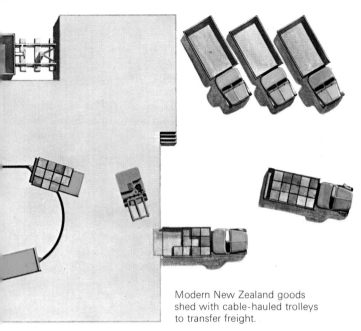

Modern New Zealand goods
shed with cable-hauled trolleys
to transfer freight.

cases, where there is a wagon load, the freight can be loaded at
once and the wagon labelled for despatch on a train going in the
right direction, if not to the nearest terminal. Part wagon loads
are more difficult and expensive to handle, but it may be
possible to group them with other freight of a suitable type
going to the same destination or in the same direction. If they
have to be carried any distance in the terminal it may be by
automatic trucks steered by a buried cable under the floor or
by moving belts. Ideally, every piece of freight would be put
in a direct through wagon, but this is impossible in practice.

For the moment, we will assume that we have an individual
wagon load for which no through train is available. This will
be sent off on a suitable train, with other wagons for the same
general direction, to an intermediate point where there is a
marshalling yard.

Marshalling yards are among the biggest and most elaborate
of railway installations, and among the most highly mechanized. They are also among the most expensive, and the object
of most railways is to have as few as possible, sending freight

by through trains wherever they can. No matter how efficient the yard, freight is not moving while it is in the yard area: it is being delayed.

The object of the marshalling yard is to collect wagons which have come from various directions and make them up into trains for their destinations or, if this is impossible because there is not enough traffic for that destination, to forward the wagons to another marshalling yard nearer the destination.

The procedure is for the train of wagons to arrive in the reception sidings at the yards where the locomotive is taken off and freed for other duties. The yard controllers want to know how the train is to be split up and to do that they must know the destination of each wagon. The make-up of the train may have been sent ahead by teleprinter, as is common in North America. If so, the way in which the train is to be split up will already have been decided and it is only necessary to check that the train conforms with the message already received. This can be done by someone walking the length of the train checking the list, but is often done by reading the wagon numbers over closed-circuit television as the train moves slowly past a camera. If the make-up of the train is not known it is usual for someone to walk down the train reading the destinations and numbers into a walkie-talkie radio or, sometimes, a tape recorder. From these lists the yard controllers work out where the wagons must be uncoupled – the 'cuts' – and to which of perhaps fifty or more sidings they must go. The 'cuts' may consist of one wagon or several together for the same destination.

The train is then pushed slowly by a radio-equipped – sometimes even radio-controlled – shunting locomotive – normally a diesel – up a slope leading to a peak called the 'hump'. On the other side the tracks drop away steeply. As the first cut comes to the crest of the hump and goes over, it gathers speed rapidly and moves away from the rest of the train. It is then directed through a maze of power-operated points, beginning with the line dividing into two (the 'king' ints) then each line into two again (the 'queen' points), and each of those into two again (the 'jack' points) and so on as required to make up the number of sidings. Before the first

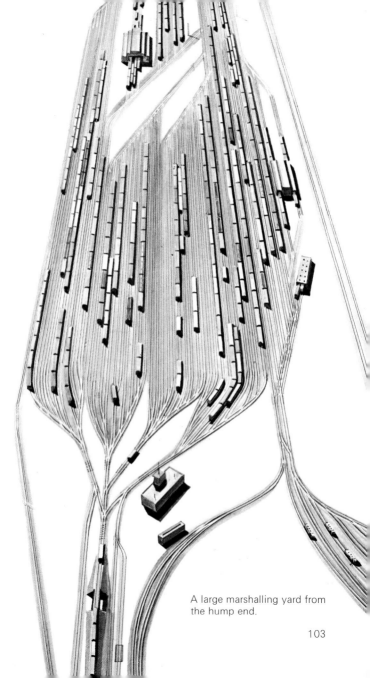

A large marshalling yard from the hump end.

cut has gone very far, the second is gathering speed and the points change quickly to divert it to the proper siding. This process goes on until all the train has been split up and the wagons are on the proper sidings.

It will be seen that the working of the points has to be smartly carried out, and this is often done mechanically or electronically, the cut' list made up from the list of wagon destinations being fed into a unit which makes the point changes automatically, changing points for the next 'cut' as soon as the preceeding one is clear. Sometimes it is done by an operator from the same type of list, using push-button controls which can usually 'store' several cuts so that the operator can work ahead of the cut coming over the hump.

With many tracks, a yard can cover a wide area – the one at Montreal, for example, has 124 sorting sidings or 'classification tracks' and can hold 11,000 wagons on its 165 miles of rails, so the distance a wagon has to run under gravity when it is pushed over the hump can vary a great deal, especially as some tracks may be empty and others nearly full. In many yards, therefore, the speed at which the cut must run is calculated by a computer which is fed automatically with information on the destination siding, the number of wagons in that siding, the curvature of the track on the route to be followed, the wind direction and pressure, and the 'rollability' of each cut, i.e. the speed at which it will roll, which depends on the condition of the wagons, the number of them, the amount of load in them and other factors. This is measured by radar as the cut rolls down the hump. The speed is then controlled by 'retarders', which press against the wheels and slow the wagons down. There are usually two sets of retarders, primary and secondary, and the pressure of both can be varied in several degrees. Recently small hydraulic piston-type

Loading piggy-back road
trailers by mobile portal crane.

retarders spread along the sidings have come into use. These
have the advantage of being able to give a push to a slow-
moving wagon as well as being able to slow down a wagon
that is moving too fast.

From the sorting sidings, wagons are hauled away to form
new trains and despatched to their destinations.

Containers, described in some detail in an earlier chapter,
can be handled at ordinary freight terminals by mobile cranes
or large fork lift trucks, the only essentials being that there
should be a suitable siding with road access and room for the
crane to manoeuvre. For full efficiency – as with the Freightliner trains – it is necessary to have special terminals.

'Kangarou' trailers being
loaded by tractor on to special
pouched wagons.

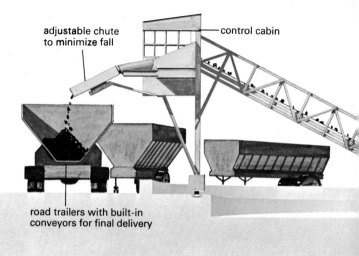

adjustable chute
to minimize fall

control cabin

road trailers with built-in
conveyors for final delivery

A Freightliner train as developed in Britain has perhaps fifteen high-speed wagons, each 62 feet 6 inches long and able to carry various combinations of containers up to nearly that length. Such a train can carry 675 tons of freight in containers and it always travels direct from terminal to terminal, an advice of its load being sent ahead.

A typical terminal may have three sidings each long enough for a whole train, i.e. something over 1,000 feet long. There will also be a heavy-duty road parallel with or between the sidings. Sidings and roadway are spanned by giant cranes able to lift the heaviest container. They are mounted on rails and able to move the full length of the sidings. Such cranes as these can make the transfer between road and rail vehicle inside two minutes. Two of them can transfer the load of a whole Freightliner train to lorries within two hours, freeing the train for reloading in the same time and enabling the best use possible to be made of the special vehicles.

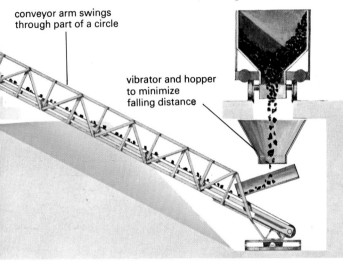

Bulk coal collection and delivery
service to coal merchants cuts
costs and eases handling.

rail wagon with bottom door

conveyor arm swings
through part of a circle

vibrator and hopper
to minimize
falling distance

The cranes are fitted with equipment enabling them to handle any of the wide range of containers used or being developed for these trains, and the advice of the load received in advance enables the right road vehicles to be ready at the proper time and in the appropriate place.

Elsewhere, 'piggy-back' vehicles are handled in much the same way, but there is an ingenious 'Flexi-Van', introduced by the New York Central and now spreading to Europe, which is rather different. This is, in effect, a container mounted on a two-axle road bogie to make it into a trailer. When it arrives at the rail terminal the road tractor backs the trailer, at right angles, against a special rail wagon and the body then slides off the bogie on to a turntable in the wagon. Once the body is on the wagon, the turntable enables one man to turn it parallel with the wagon for its rail journey.

Road trailers are backed over a dock or up a special ramp on to the end of a train of flat wagons, the gaps between wagon

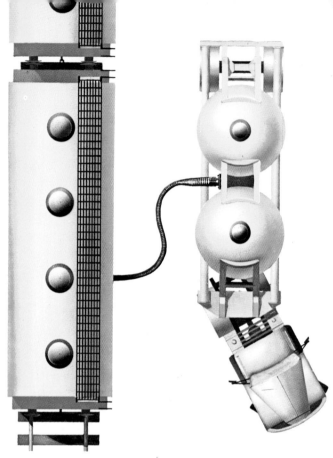

Transferring cement in bulk from rail tanker to road vehicle by air pressure. Below: a refrigerator wagon for international traffic.

ends being bridged by metal plates. Once the trailer is fastened securely the tractor can drive off to fetch another trailer. With the French 'Kangarou' and other low-height systems, the trailer wheels are loaded onto the wagon by a tractor and guided into special slots below the level of the wagon frame.

The handling of some bulk freight has already been mentioned, but there are others which also need special terminals, large or small, such as petrol, oil and lubricants, which need storage tanks, pipelines and pumps to deliver oil into railway tank wagons or pump it out. Milk in bulk needs something very similar. Bulk grain and cement and powders need silos and ducts, and the powders often a compressed air supply to load and unload their special wagons and containers. Refrigerated traffic may need a special cold storage terminal, or power or fuelling facilities to keep refrigerating equipment at work while the wagon is standing.

One of the problems in countries using domestic solid fuels is to distribute the coal, coke, etc., economically to small merchants or fairly small-scale users. An ingenious answer is the centralized coal distribution terminal, which takes block trains of hopper wagons direct from a colliery and unloads them into a shallow hopper below the tracks feeding a belt system capable of being rotated through a quarter-circle. The belt passes along a jib-type arm, raising the coal to a height sufficient to serve a delivery chute suspended above a waiting road vehicle. The road vehicles are thirteen-ton capacity hopper semi-trailers which can be hauled by tractor to the final delivery point where, using built-in conveyors of their own, they can stack the coal where it is required. A terminal such as this one eliminates the need for small railway-served coal yards over a wide area and makes possible a more intensive use of wagons.

The hopper wagon used in coal trains is itself a specialized vehicle, as is the refrigerated car, but there are many other examples. Although the wagon came before the container, in many ways the specialized wagon now takes over from the specialized container when the flow of traffic grows large enough to warrant it. To take another type of bulk load, for example – motor cars from the factory: special double-deck (and even triple-deck in the U.S.A.) vehicles are used every-

where to deliver new motor cars to large distributors. Each of
the special wagons takes anything from six to twelve or more
motor cars and a train of these car transporters is an impressive
sight. There are other wagons with opening roofs and opening
sides designed to allow mechanical loading from above or
fork-lift loading from the sides. Large light alloy wagons carry
huge loads of alumina – one type of fifteen-ton wagon in
France can carry sixty-five tons of this oxide. There are long
low wagons, sometimes with a well in the middle between the
bogies, for heavy loads; special wagons which open in the
centre or have roll-back roofs for various loads, sometimes
fitted or compartmented to take, say, coiled tinplate. All these
and many more have their place, but all demand terminals
adapted for their needs with the right equipment to deal with
them. A hopper wagon with bottom doors which will release
the load in seconds is useless without a special storage hopper
beneath the track to receive that load. There is, however,
a wagon used in Germany that is capable of tipping from one

Special wagon with opening top
for carrying heavy coils of steel
plate safe from the weather.

end or to either side, thus simplifying the whole problem.

Because most freight (apart from private siding traffic) must begin and finish its journey by road, and the most difficult part of the operation is loading, unloading, and transferring goods, it is self-evident that it does not matter a great deal if the goods spend another half-hour on the road vehicle if this can speed up the overall time of transit. The tendency is therefore to have fewer and fewer terminals, but to equip those terminals with every modern freight-handling device. When the number is reduced drastically, as in some countries it has been, the number of trains that can be sent directly from terminal to terminal without passing through a marshalling yard is greatly increased, and the time of the journey is reduced by hours – or even days – accordingly. As with the coal distribution terminal, each freight terminal is equipped with road vehicles which range over a wide area. In this way the railways can provide a much better and quicker service than if the rails served every village individually.

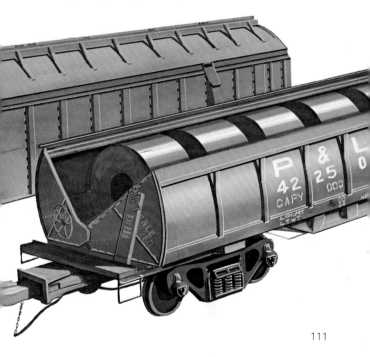

Trains for Towns

The world's first city underground railway was opened in London in 1863 mainly because of the traffic congestion in the city's streets. Today traffic congestion is still the mainspring of many new schemes for urban, underground or rapid transit railways.

The first $3\frac{3}{4}$-mile London rapid transit railway, the Metropolitan, running from Bishop's Road, Paddington, to Farringdon Street, was worked by steam trains, and a grimy, sulphurous affair it must have been at times. It was, however, quick and, as far as its carriages were concerned, comfortable. Londoners flocked to it, over 26,000 passengers a day using it in the first month of its existence. It was soon followed by the Metropolitan District Railway, also steam operated and also popular. It was not until 1890, that the deep, shield-driven, electrically-operated 'tube' railway came to London with tiny

London Underground train in the days of steam.

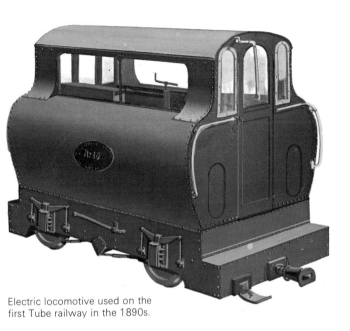

Electric locomotive used on the
first Tube railway in the 1890s.

four-wheeled 100 h.p. electric locomotives drawing almost
windowless cars. This was the City & South London Railway,
the forerunner of the tube railways which with the Metropolitan, District and Circle sub-surface lines, now give the
quickest means of travelling across the metropolitan area.

Although London had a long start, the advantages of rail-
ways through city centres were not lost on other cities.
Glasgow opened a cable-hauled subway in 1896, Paris its first
Metro in 1900, Berlin its 'Kellerbahn' (cellar railway) in 1902,
Hamburg in 1912, Rome in 1955, Milan in 1964, Madrid in
1919, Rotterdam in 1968, Stockholm in 1950, Moscow in 1935,
Leningrad in 1955, Kiev in 1960, New York in 1904, Toronto
in 1954, Tokyo in 1927, and so on – there are many others.
This miscellany of geography and dates shows that the virtues
of rapid transit are and have been recognized all over the
world for at least sixty years.

The London Metropolitan Railway was built largely by a
process of opening up a huge trench and then roofing it in. It
is comparatively simple to do if one can uproot whatever there

may be above for a considerable period. The resulting lines are shallow – just below the surface – and easily and quickly reached by short staircases.

In London some lines are much deeper down and have to be built with tunnelling shields – basically a steel cylinder pushed along through the earth on its side by hydraulic rams, making a shelter for men who dig away the earth with pneumatic tools. As the shield is pushed forward into the gap thus made, the section of tunnel behind is immediately lined with cast iron or concrete tunnel segments. Many shields have mechanical cutting apparatus inside them and can work much more quickly than with hand-tool methods. A speed of $4\frac{1}{2}$ft an hour has been reached, in blue clay, when constructing new

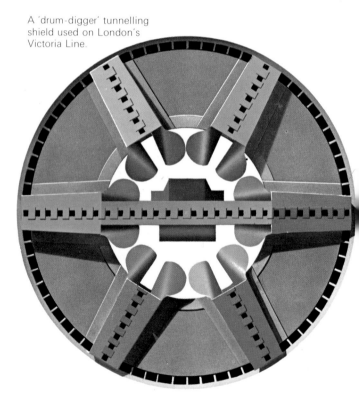

A 'drum-digger' tunnelling shield used on London's Victoria Line.

Line by using one of these modern tunnelling shields.

Largely because of the spread of the motor car, rapid transit in the 1960s is enjoying a remarkable world-wide boom which is at its height in the U.S.A., the home of the motor car. This is because planners, administrators and engineers realized that their cities would gradually become concrete deserts if enough roads were to be built to take the ever-increasing flood of cars. Their warnings were taken up by city after city and in 1964 President Johnson signed an important measure, the Urban Mass Transportation Act, which authorized Federal grants of two-thirds of the cost of approved transit improvements, provided that, among other things, the proposals were part of a comprehensive scheme for the

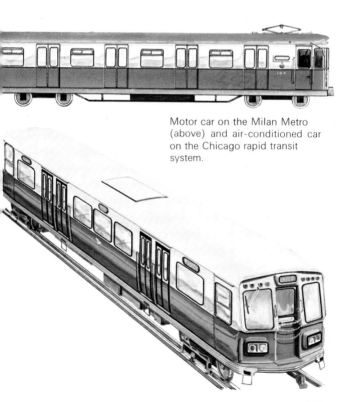

Motor car on the Milan Metro (above) and air-conditioned car on the Chicago rapid transit system.

redevelopment and transportation of a complete area.

The promise of federal funds on this scale opened the flood-gates, and nearly every large city in the U.S.A. is now improving any rapid transit facilities it has or is planning to build systems to serve the city and its surroundings. There are networks in New York, Chicago, Philadelphia, Boston and Cleveland. New systems which are fast and efficient have been built in Washington and San Francisco.

San Francisco is especially important because its Bay Area Rapid Transit District started from scratch, refusing to take anything for granted, and carried out substantial studies and tests of almost everything concerned with rapid transit. The conclusion they reached was that an electric railway, with steel wheels on steel rails, was better for their 75-mile rapid transit system than rubber-tyred trains or monorails. Their system also includes automatically-operated trains, automatic fare collection, and many other advanced features.

Part of the San Francisco line runs in the dividing strip between the twin carriageways of motor roads, a promising

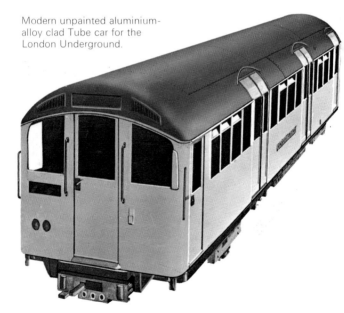

Modern unpainted aluminium-alloy clad Tube car for the London Underground.

Train on the Lisbon Metropolitano railway.

practice also followed by some sections of the Chicago system. When motorway and railway are built together in the same operation there are advantages to both.

To woo the commuter away from his motor car, the rapid transit planners are designing high-speed vehicles which will have comfort almost unknown for this type of travel, with carpeted floors, luxury seating and air conditioning.

Overall planning for transit is usually in the hands of a rapid transit district or a metropolitan transit authority, many of which have been created recently. In some cases they also control the suburban services of the main-line railways. Some of the new lines are being planned to be partly in tunnel, partly on the surface and partly on 'aerial structures'. In San Francisco, for example, the BARTD scheme has twenty miles in tunnels of various sorts – including a four-mile sunken tube across San Francisco Bay – and thirty-one miles on aerial structures, the remaining twenty-four miles being on the surface. Even the London Underground, with its shallow covered ways and deep tubes, is not what its name implies, for it has only a third or so of its system under the ground.

Rubber-tyred train with guide
wheels on the Montreal Metro.

In Europe, rapid transit railways have usually – though not
always – had the support of the city, the regional government,
and the state, so activity has not been suddenly re-born as in
the U.S.A. but has been a steady progress interrupted mainly
by the two world wars. Nevertheless, activity there is. In
London, the new Dockland Light Railway connects the
recently developed Dockland area in East London to the city.
In Paris, a new deep-level double-track tube for main-line size
trains has been built to run east and west below the city, with
interchange stations for the Metro and connections with the
French main-line railways at each end. The West Berlin
underground is extending its lines; Rotterdam has opened its
first rapid transit line, partly in tunnel, partly on a bridge
across the Nieuwe Maas and partly elevated; Munich built its
first underground line for the Olympics of 1972; Budapest has
new deep lines and has plans for others. Prague and Warsaw
are building as is Vienna, which already has a light underground railway – the Stadtbahn. Germany also has a number of
sub-surface lines under constuction which are designed to take
underground trains eventually but will be worked by
tramcars, or trains of tramcars, until traffic grows enough to
justify full-size rapid transit trains. There are similar lines in
Belgium.

In Russia, Moscow and Leningrad are extending their systems steadily and there are new lines in Kiev, Tbilisi and Baku: Kharkov and Tashkent are among the newcomers to the rapid transit field.

Rome has a small modern system which it is expanding and Milan has very sophisticated lines which are being followed by others. Lisbon, Madrid – unique in having four peak hours a day because so many people go home for lunch – and Barcelona, all have their own lines and all are anxious to expand them. In the north, Oslo and Stockholm have rapid transit lines, and Helsinki bids soon to join them. In South America, Buenos Aires has long had an efficient and busy system. In Japan, Tokyo has a rapidly-expanding network, as has Osaka, the second largest city: Nagoya also has a small but swiftly-growing system. Places which are taking their first steps into the ranks of rapid transit cities, either building or with plans include Lyons, Melbourne, Sydney, Auckland, Wellington, Johannesburg, Bombay, Calcutta, Delhi, Hong Kong, Cairo, Teheran, Istanbul, Tel-Aviv, Sao Paulo, Lima, Caracas and Kobe.

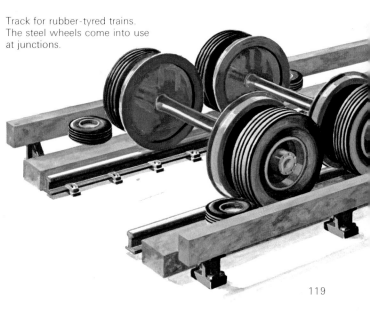

Track for rubber-tyred trains. The steel wheels come into use at junctions.

The rubber-tyred trains noted a number of times already were first used on the Paris Metro, where several lines are equipped with them. The rubber-tyred wheels of the cars run on concrete tracks and they are steered by horizontal wheels pressing against side guides in the tunnels. Should a tyre burst, the bogie sinks slightly and allows normal railway wheels, attached to the same axles as the rubber-tyred ones, to drop down on to conventional rails laid alongside the concrete strips. At points and crossings the strips sink away, leaving the train to negotiate the points on railway wheels like a normal train. Because the lines take so long to convert to this complicated track, the Paris Metro reverted to steel wheels on steel rails for some of its stock. Apart from Paris, rubber-tyred trains of this type run in Montreal, on the Haifa underground funicular railway and on the new line in Mexico City. Santiago also uses these trains.

Rapid transit railways are always seeking to reduce recurring costs, such as heavy bills for labour, so they are in the forefront of experiments in automation. Automatic fare collection is one of the main subjects for experiment at present,

Station on the new San Francisco system, with automatic fare collection gates and air-conditioned train.

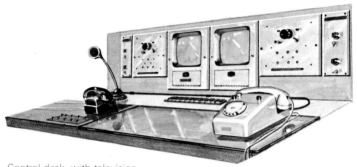

Control desk, with television
monitors, at Milan Metro station.

and trials are going on in the U.S.A., Japan, Britain and Europe.
Many passengers using the London Underground now have
weekly, monthly or yearly travelcards for convenience and
these tickets cover all tube, bus and rail travel in a given area
for the duration of the card. The passenger can buy his ticket
from a clerk or from a machine selling the value of ticket, which
may also give change. Now there are also machines which will
give a whole range of tickets and change, as well as machines to
change notes for coins of convenient value.

In the latest systems, the ticket is coded by punched holes
or by imposing on it a magnetic pattern, and forms a key to

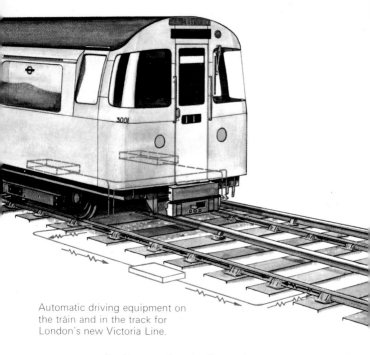

Automatic driving equipment on the train and in the track for London's new Victoria Line.

open a gate leading to the platform, the gate returning the ticket as the passenger passes through. At the end of his journey a similar gate, linked usually to a small local or large central computer, 'reads' the ticket and decides whether the right fare has been paid, whether the ticket has the proper date, or, for a season ticket, whether it is valid at that station and is still current. This entails the gate searching through its electronic memory for the fares from, sometimes, a couple of hundred stations. An ordinary ticket is retained by the gate at the destination station, but a season is returned. An incorrect ticket will not open the gates and the passenger must go to the station staff. London's Victoria Line and the San Francisco system were among the first lines to have automatic fare collection with fares related to distance.

The station staff may consist of one man, as in Milan, where there is a flat-fare system. He sits in a booth and examines season tickets. He also watches the platforms through closed-circuit television, makes loud-speaker announcements and watches that all is well. In emergency, he can cut off the current from the tracks.

In Paris, London, Berlin, Moscow, Leningrad, Hamburg, New York, Barcelona, Stockholm and elsewhere great strides have been made with automatic train operation, in which trains either pick up commands by induction from trackside cables or the track itself, or have a 'programme' on board designed to cause them to run under power, coast, or brake according to the characteristics of the journey between any two stations. There are also safeguards against the presence of a train ahead. Paris has lines under automatic operation, as has Barcelona. London has a five-station branch line working automatically, and the Victoria Line works in exactly the same way. Another method, adopted for San Francisco, is to bring all trains under the control of a central computer. So far, automatically-driven trains all carry a train operator who starts the train and can take over in emergency.

Automatic driving system as tested in New York.

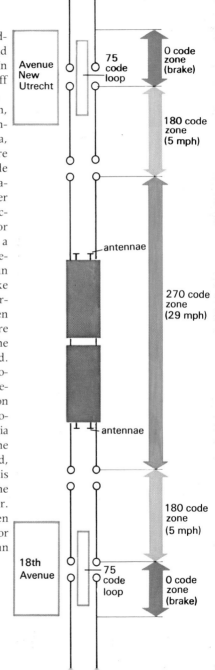

The Rail Way Ahead

What is to be the role of the railway in the future? Is it to remain one of the world's primary means of transport? If so, what will it be like and what traffic will it carry?

The railway is likely to remain as a vital highway for many years yet. Recent detailed appraisals have shown that steel wheels on steel rails are capable of much more than was at one time thought possible. Only a few years ago 125 m.p.h. was regarded as the upper limit of speed on conventional track, but 200–236 m.p.h. has now been shown to be possible in regular service provided that the track is carefully laid – in particular, carefully levelled – and well maintained. This means that the 'competition distance' between railways and aircraft can be lengthened considerably, especially if it is a good many years before VTOL aircraft can land nearer city centres and the city-airport journey remains relatively slow.

Canadian National Railways
revolutionary new Turbo-Train
for fast services.

Passenger comfort will need special attention if the high-speed trains are to keep their clientele. Ordinary luxury-hotel comforts of seating, food, air-conditioning, and a general high standard of train appointments can be taken for granted, but there will have to be a considerable rebuilding and easing of curves on high-speed lines to protect passengers from the effects of centrifugal force. There is a limit to what can be done by 'superelevation', i.e. raising the outer rail to bank the train as it goes round curves – the train may have to stop on those curves or go round them slowly at times. There is a possibility that new types of suspension which will allow the body of the carriage to move independently of the frame may relieve some of these effects, but they have yet to be tried on a wide scale. It is necessary to build new main lines to reach the highest standards. Even the superb standards and 8,200 foot radius curves of the new Tokaido Line in Japan are not thought good enough, and its extension is being built to yet higher standard. It is a measure of the Japanese faith in high-speed railways in their crowded islands that it is being built at all, but it is being vindicated by government-assisted work in the U.S.A. on creating a high-speed railway route along the whole length of the Boston–New York–Washington corridor. Another point to be watched is the sudden and disconcerting rise of air pressure as a high-speed train enters a tunnel. Only a sealed train can obviate this, but it might be possible to close all vents automatically at the tunnel approach.

As train speeds rise so does the power needed to operate them, so that careful attention will have to be paid to the

aerodynamic shape of the front end of trains, to a generally smooth surface without breaks, and to light but strong methods of construction. These can bring the requirements down to reasonable levels which can be supplied by electric or diesel power. Though the new small gas turbines offer considerable promise, it is probable that the new railways will be electrically powered with motors spread out along the train. This is because electricity can be generated from several types of fuel or water power, and also because electric motors are capable of giving out much more than their rated power for short periods – valuable in initial acceleration. Electric motors also enable rheostatic or regenerative braking to be used in a speed range where present braking methods, except disc brakes, are likely to fail from overheating.

The new electric railways already exist in the 320-mile New Tokaido line in Japan and its 350-mile extension to Hakata, in the British London-Liverpool-Manchester line (not as fast as the New Tokaido but nevertheless of a very high standard) and the considerably improved New York–Washington tracks picked as the high-speed test grounds of the state-backed electrical trial services.

The new turbines are also well advanced. The Canadian National Turbo-Trains mentioned elsewhere have not altogether lived up to expectations, but the French have very successful high-speed turbine trains in service and the British 'Advanced Passenger Train' (APT) has attracted a great deal of international attention. It is expected to reduce the weight per passenger to only 40 per cent of that of a conventional train and to be capable of 150 m.p.h. or more. Even more important than the top speed is the expected very rapid acceleration and deceleration possible with this train. A hydraulic system will control banking on curves to enable them to be taken faster and newly-developed running gear gives a steering action which will take the train through curves without the wheel flanges grinding on the rails and causing wear and tear. The deceleration is obtained from a new form of hydraulic braking which will be so effective that in many cases new signalling will not be needed, since the train will be able to stop within the limits now allowed. Whether this high rate of deceleration will be within the limits of reasonable passenger toleration remains to be seen. It is not difficult with conventional methods – boldly applied – to stop a train smartly, but only by flinging passengers about. A smooth deceleration is what is needed and British Rail seem to have found it.

This train relies on aircraft techniques for both bodies and engines, and in time orders for it could well go to aircraft manufacturers already familiar with these techniques as well as the traditional railway rolling stock builders. The train is on the rails and showing its paces and production models are on the way. Some form of automatic control seems essential at these speeds, and no doubt some special devices – perhaps new,

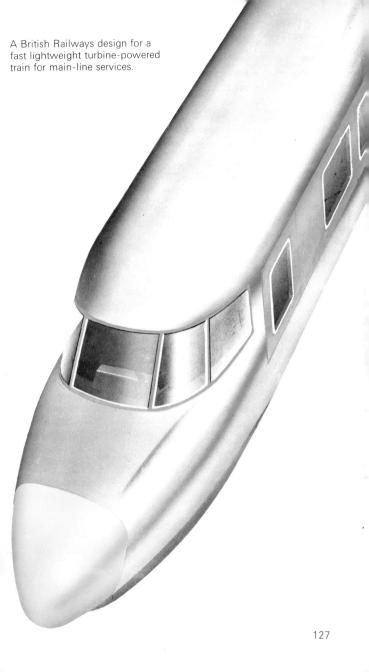

A British Railways design for a fast lightweight turbine-powered train for main-line services.

perhaps versions of equipment already in use or under trial – could fit the circumstances.

As far as freight is concerned, speed will not need – at least at first – to be quite as high and locomotives will probably be the best form of power, though permanent-set trains of the Freightliner type could well be multiple-units with dispersed motors. The aim will certainly be to run freight trains direct from terminal to terminal at the highest speed possible, and the closer this speed approaches that of the passenger trains the better, for the new, expensive railway tracks will need to be intensively used if they are to be economic, with as many trains as possible channelled on to them. The nearer to a uniform speed the trains can achieve, the more that can run over one pair of rails. The faster the speed of all types of trains, the more journeys each train can make. In this way fewer trains can do more work and reduce capital costs.

When the New Tokaido Line was built it was fully intended that it should be used for freight as well as passenger trains, with the freight trains taking only $5\frac{1}{2}$ hours to run between Tokyo and Osaka. Goods would have been loaded in containers and carried on specially-built multiple-unit trains designed to carry containers and including most of the features of the passenger stock. The maximum speed would have been 81 m.p.h. against the 125 m.p.h. intended at that time for passenger trains on the same line.

In fact, the freight trains have never been built, so we have

been denied the experience of operating super-fast trains for goods alone, but there is little doubt that this is the direction in which things are moving. If not the New Tokaido, some other line will eventually be moving freight at up to 100 m.p.h.

At high speeds, human reactions become too slow to be entirely trusted unless all operators have the same physical standards as racing drivers or airline pilots. This means, in effect, that the trains will have to have automatic safeguards built-in to them and at anything over 130–150 m.p.h. they ought to be entirely automatically controlled. Fortunately, the railway lends itself ideally to automation. It runs on a fixed, predictable track of steel, a material through which electric currents can flow or in which they can be induced. Already speed controls can be imposed on trains from central super-vision rooms and systems of full automatic driving have been developed for rapid transit trains which could readily be adapted for main-line use. The uniform running character-istics which such a system imposes will help to make the greatest possible use of the lines – making two tracks, perhaps, do the work done by four today.

To take account of the variations of traffic inevitable when freight and passenger trains are run on the same lines, it is probable that a central computer may be used to watch the running of trains on the whole line, imposing its commands over those given automatically to the train by the signalling system – which will be controlled by the train ahead – and

A British Railways Freightliner train on its fast inter-city run laden with containers.

over any driving commands given from the trackside or by a train-borne operating programme'. An automatic, track-guided radar system will warn trains of obstruction on the line from non-railway causes, e.g. a crashed road vehicle which has rolled on to the track.

In this way the railways could be, indeed are slowly being, changed into a high-capital, low labour-cost industry in which individual employees will be highly-paid and highly skilled. Passenger trains will probably need a human operator for many years if only to reassure passengers, but freight trains will probably run without anyone on board. Stations will need very few staff because ticket-selling and collecting will be entirely automatic and much of the present bustle of large stations will be obviated by putting mail and luggage into small containers or pallets which can be loaded and unloaded swiftly by a mechanical truck. Parcels will probably have their own trains on busy routes and elsewhere they will be pallet-ized. There will be many fewer stations, and possibly passengers, like freight, will be taken to and distributed from provincial stations by road services – as they are to air terminals from cities.

Bulk traffics will travel in block trains, as many do today, but it is likely that coal traffic, which has been the mainstay of British Railways as well as, by its sheer quantity, one of the greatest stumbling blocks to technical progress, will be gradually reduced and eventually die in many areas. The coal traffic that remains is likely to be between pits and industrial users, making for highly-mechanized, swift and economical transport.

Short-range or commuter transport is likely to become still more important as populations rise and people tend more and more to gravitate towards built-up areas, turning neighbouring cities into giant conurbations. The growth of purely urban, or rapid transit lines can be taken for granted, the process of planning and building them is already well under way, but what are now the suburban and outer suburban lines of the main line railways are likely to undergo a change of some magnitude.

For shorter suburban trips commuter trains are likely to get nearer and nearer in design to those of rapid transit railways.

Speed, space and comfort—the attributes of modern railways.

Automobile transport, stacked three high, in the U.S.A.

Like them, they will probably be automatically driven with a one-man supervisor as crew, have a fairly small proportion of seats to total capacity, and plenty of standing space. Automatic door operation is already in use on some suburban trains in various parts of the world: it is likely to be adopted for all of them. With increasing road congestion, stations on such lines could well get nearer together rather than further apart, making it possible for all commuters to walk to their local stations. This in turn could lead to provision of express lanes on the railways so that a train could pick up at a group of stations and then run fast to the centre. With modern signalling and the trend towards shorter but higher peaks, this type of working might be possible by using both railway tracks one way on the tidal-flow principle, one as the pick-up route and the other as the fast, but this would only be possible if stabling space for trains were available at the centre and trains did not have to make a swift return trip for another load of passengers. In such cases extra tracks would be needed. Passengers travelling in small numbers against the peak flow might even be catered for by road transport, with which the railways should have close liaison, including inter-available tickets. Where a rapid transit railway system exists there should be some through running of trains, as in Tokyo, which means there should be common loading gauges, common standards of current supply and automatic operating systems capable of controlling both types of train. Suburban lines would obviously need to be completely segregated from the high-speed main lines.

Some outer-suburban traffic, which even today can mean distances of up to 100 miles or so, could be put on the high-speed lines. The rest would be in comfortable trains with a high proportion of seats which would serve fairly widely spaced stations at first, switching to the fast suburban track at an interchange station on the edge of the inner suburban area and not calling at the closely-spaced stations. Suburban stations could be one- or two-man operated and should serve as centres for feeder bus routes.

Careful thought will have to be given to the role of the bus in relation to railways. Even now, as non-paying branch lines cease to operate, buses are taking their place. Just as buses feed urban railway stations, so these longer-distance vehicles feed the main lines. But there are coaches which will pick the passenger up in his village and take him all the way to his destination much more cheaply, if more slowly, than the bus and train together. Good as railway services may be, fares must also be watched very carefully.

Trains for Special Jobs

The role of the railway in logistics has been discussed in an earlier chapter, but many of the trains involved in wars have been designed for other purposes than the carrying of troops and stores. During the last war many trains were used to carry tanks from manufacturers to depots, but they were also used in the operational movement of squadrons and regiments of tanks from one front to another in Europe and in the movement of operational units from one area to another out of the line of battle. For such operational moves flat wagons were used with bridge pieces covering the end gaps between wagons. The tank squadron would drive straight on to the end of the train, much as motor cars do now, the leading tank going to the far end and the rest taking up position along the train behind. The task of the leader, with the driver of the huge vehicle peering out through a small slit, was not enviable, and many tanks must have gone over the side or end of the train until the operation became familiar through practice.

Where military trains are moved through a conquered but still hostile countryside, or where raiding parties from the other side can be expected, the war-time railway needs protection by constant patrol against sabotage or ambush. Even in the days of the Sudan campaigns, the railway which carried troops through the desert had trains headed by armoured and heavily armed wagons that were pushed ahead of the locomotive, keeping a sharp watch for damaged track or enemies in waiting.

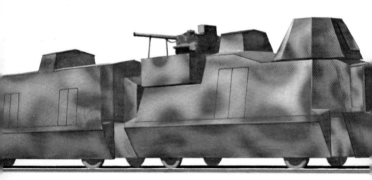

Similar heavily-protected wagons were used in the American Civil War, sometimes as patrol vehicles and sometimes as mobile blockhouses to guard bridges or other strategic points. In the last war German anti-sabotage measures in the occupied countries included armoured trains which were virtually land battleships, armoured swivelling gun turrets not excluded.

Massive wagons have been used by several countries as bases for long-range guns, the only way to move these huge guns to their firing area being by rail. To prevent the enemy pin-pointing them and destroying them by gunfire or bombing from the air, they were frequently moved to new positions, special sidings being built for them almost overnight. This role is now transferred to various forms of missile, which also can be mounted on suitable rail chassis. With the longer range of modern missiles the railway is perhaps even more useful than before for such weapons. Incidentally, the bombing raids of the last war showed quite clearly that it is a fallacy to think that a railway can be knocked out for long by bombing only. Emergency repairs can be made so quickly, once the right organization is set up, that trains can be on their way again in a matter of hours after any ordinary incident.

Rockets are also used to propel vehicles on the fastest railways in the world, the sledge tracks built in the U.S.A. to test ultrasonic aircraft and spacecraft equipment. There are quite a number of these, and they are true railways, sometimes even of standard gauge, built to fine precision limits. The actual speeds reached are not disclosed, but the Supersonic Naval Ordnance Research Track (SNORT) at China Lake was known

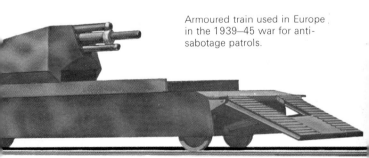

Armoured train used in Europe in the 1939–45 war for anti-sabotage patrols.

to have held the world's land speed record until 1959 – what may have happened in recent years is anybody's guess. The sleds, carrying aircraft fuselages, parts of spacecraft, and so on, ride on metal shoes gliding on the top of the rail. To prevent the sled leaving the track there are small slippers which ride beneath the overhang of the rail head on each side. The sleds, having been rapidly accelerated by rockets up to high speed for the tests, are slowed down by running through shallow water or dragging a scoop through a water trough. The last two miles of the SNORT track can be flooded as required to various depths.

One of the disadvantages of railways, as we have seen earlier, is that smooth steel wheels on smooth steel rails do not get a good enough grip to climb steep hills. Yet railways do climb hills, and can climb more steeply than any road vehicle, given the right conditions.

The steepest gradient operated by unaided wheels, i.e. by adhesion alone, is 1 in 11 on the metre-gauge Chamonix line between Chedde and Servoz: this is an electrified line operated by the French National Railways. To allow still steeper slopes to be climbed, a toothed wheel is fitted below the power car or locomotive of the train. The teeth on this wheel engage in teeth cut into the edge of a metal bar, or rail, which is fastened on

edge between the running rails with the teeth upward. This gives a non-slip grip to the toothed wheel, which is driven by the motors of the train in the usual way. One of the most commonly-used systems – it is used for the Pike's Peak line in the U.S.A., the Snowdon Mountain Railway in Britain, and many Swiss mountain railways – is the Abt, which has two toothed rails side-by-side but staggered so that the teeth of one come opposite the gaps in the other. There are also two toothed driving pinions, similarly staggered. In this way the grip is doubly secure as well as being smooth and constant. For the railway up Mount Pilatus in Switzerland, which in places is as steep as 1 in 2, a special rack was devised by Dr Locher, Engineer of the line. There is a flat metal bar laid between the running rails with teeth cut in both sides, and the cars have pinions mounted in pairs with the rack rail between them. This not only gives a positive grip but also centres the cars on the track so that flanges on the running wheels are not necessary. This makes it easier for the cars to follow the very sharp curves on the line.

There are even steeper railways, known as funiculars, on which the cars are hauled up by cables. There are usually two cars, one ascending and one descending, on opposite ends of the same cable so that the weight of one balances the other.

The U.S. Navy SNORT rocket sled track for aircraft testing.

This type of line can be worked by water power, the descending car having a large underfloor tank which is filled with water at the top of the slope to increase its weight, so that it can pull the other car up. The tank is emptied when the car reaches the bottom while the tank on the upper car is filled. Alternatively, the railway can be worked by power winding mechanism. Such lines can be very steep indeed. One in Switzerland, between Piotta and Piora, climbs at 1 in $1\frac{1}{8}$, that is, the car moves 1 foot upwards for every 1 foot $1\frac{1}{2}$ inches that it moves forwards.

Montmartre funicular railway
up the hill to the famous
Paris church of Sacré Coeur.

Monorails have been much in the news recently, although the first one was built as early as 1824 and had been patented three years before that. It seems almost a symbol of modernity among city planners to advocate that a monorail system should be built to carry passengers above the streets. Fortunately, the days when monorails were depicted as careering across the sky on a rail as thin as a piece of string, without any thought of weight, centrifugal force, or even power supply, have gone. The monorails being presented as serious propositions today are sound engineering jobs depicted in a responsible way.

There are two main types of monorail contending for interest today. Neither of them is a true monorail in the sense of balancing above one rail – though such cars *have* been built in the past. The most successful monorail at present, in terms of lines built and working, is the Alweg. This is a supported

Electric rack locomotive pushing
its train up a mountain slope.

type, which means that the rail, which takes the form of a concrete beam on edge, is underneath the cars. The cars sit above the rail and are supported by rubber-tyred driving wheels which run on the top edge of the beam. They are held upright and guided by horizontal rubber-tyred wheels running on formed surfaces near the top and bottom of the beam sides. Along the 'web' of the beam, between the upper and lower tyre tracks, is the power feed. There are Alweg-type lines – mostly short ones – in the U.S.A. and Japan, with an eight-mile line between Tokyo and its airport which has shown the possibilities of this type of line for airport services. Because it is paralleled by a fast motorway, however, the line has been denied the financial success which had been hoped for it.

The other type of monorail, the French Safege, is rather different. The wheels, rubber-tyred again, are mounted on bogies which run inside a box girder. The girder has a slit in the bottom surface through which pass supports for the car itself, which hangs below. This is a good example of the suspended monorail, though in fact the wheels run on surfaces on both sides of the slit in the girder so technically this is not a monorail. A trial line in France attracts many visitors.

Either supported or suspended monorails could be built down the centre of wide streets high above the traffic, and some have been built in the past only to fade away again, almost without trace. One which has not faded away is the suspended Wuppertal line in Germany, more than eight miles long, which has been working successfully since 1901. Built to solve a space problem in the narrow valley, it runs for much of its length above the River Wupper and for the rest above a main road.

A curious but very successful type of train running on the Spanish railways is the 'Talgo', which is made up of small two-wheeled cars, the front of each being articulated to the rear of the one ahead. The wheels are placed beneath the articulated joins. 'Talgo' comes from the words 'Train Articulé Léger Goicoechea et Oriel', the names being those of the inventor and his financial partner respectively. As is implied, the train is lightly built using aircraft and automobile techniques. In effect, the frames of the cars form a series of triangles which automatically follow one another as they are hauled along, so that the wheels are guided by the car ahead as well as by their flanges.

After extensive trials, the first Talgo train went into service

Alweg-type six-car monorail train in Japan.

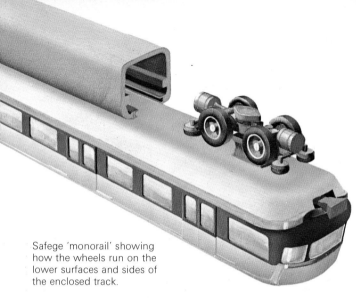

Safege 'monorail' showing
how the wheels run on the
lower surfaces and sides of
the enclosed track.

between Madrid and Hendaye in 1950. It proved particularly
suitable for this steeply-graded run through the mountains
from the Spanish capital to the French frontier. Hauled by a
specially-designed diesel locomotive, it cut the journey time
from almost twelve hours to under $8\frac{1}{2}$. It also gave a high
standard of comfort, with meals served aircraft fashion at
seats, and air-conditioning. Though trials of a Talgo-type train
in the U.S.A. proved abortive, Spain has taken to the Talgo
and many of the country's best and fastest trains are now of
this type.

Finally, an automatic railway whose cars have run more
than fifty million miles is the two-foot gauge Post Office
railway in London. Opened in 1927, it has carried mails day
and night through its $6\frac{1}{2}$ miles of deep tube tunnels ever since,
and all in trains which have no-one on board to drive or
supervise. The forty trains, the Post Office say, take the place
of 1,700 vans running on the congested London streets. To
avoid accidents, the cars, which run at up to 35 m.p.h.,
automatically cut off current from the section immediately
behind them. Special track circuiting stops them just before
they reach stations and brings them in at low speed. Brussels
has a still smaller, seven-inch gauge automatic railway

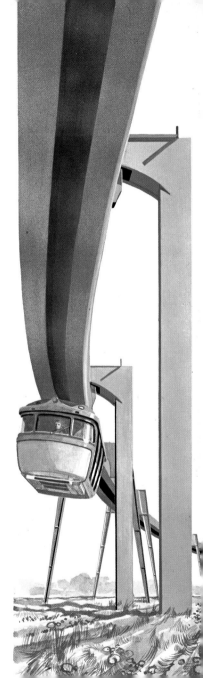

1,250 feet long. There is only one car and it works in conjunction with three lifts, all operating entirely automatically to preset instructions. A railway is usually thought of as a permanent thing – the very name 'permanent way' for the track speaks of the fixed nature of the way, but in fact there are many light railways – and monorails – which carry heavy loads and stand up to rugged treatment.

Mine railways come partly into this category, but they are often permanent in the main tunnels to the shafts and temporary only at the end near the working face, this stretch becoming gradually more permanent as working proceeds. There are also the quite large light railways in brickfields, bringing the material into the works from the giant excavation around. These are sometimes locomotive worked, but often the skips are hauled by cable. Here again, the main 'home run' tends to be permanent and the 'cutting end' temporary.

A form of monorail for freight is in worldwide use –

Safege monorail test track at Chateauneuf-sur-Loire. The car can carry 125 people at 62 m.p.h.

the Mono-Rail transporter, which can often be seen carrying material round large building sites. The cars – power wagons and trailers – run on the top of a single deep rail and have supporting wheels and rollers running on each side of the rail for guidance and support. The rails can be moved easily and the small trains, with a petrol engine or an electric motor, can surmount considerable gradients and sharp curves. Automatic controls make it possible for the train to be started from the trackside, to run until stopped by trackside controls.

The system is versatile and can be used for all kinds of purposes apart from building work – for example, carrying pipes along a pipeline from a store yard to the point where the line is being built, or for agricultural purposes.

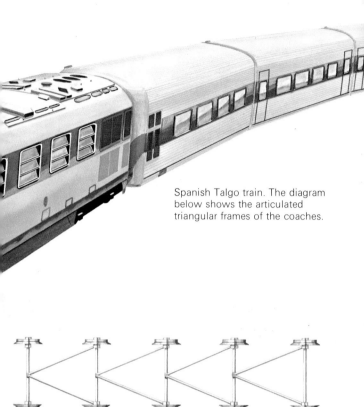

Spanish Talgo train. The diagram
below shows the articulated
triangular frames of the coaches.

A railway has even been used as an aircraft launching
catapult in the U.S.A., where special electric railways were
laid down at two airfields. The aircraft were mounted on or
towed by a rail car which carried the primary windings of an
electric motor, the secondary winding being laid out along the
whole length of the track. The track was 1,370 feet long and
the car reached 220 m.p.h.

In 1968 a new railway with only two cars opened at
Ronquières in Belgium. Each 'car' is a huge cable-hauled tank
running on four lines of rails and big enough to hold a 1,350-ton
motor barge floating in a lock-like compartment. The tanks
carry the barges from one level to another of the Charleroi-
Brussels canal.

The Future – Trains Without Rails?

A train is essentially a string of vehicles moving together – a single car, though it runs on a railway, is not strictly a train – and it is possible to have a train without having a railway.

In the search for low-friction track, locomotives were built to run on ice. One such steam locomotive was built by Nathaniel Grew in 1860 and sent to Moscow to haul freight on sledges across frozen lakes. It had driving wheels fitted with steel spikes and the front and back were supported on sledges. The front sledge could be turned by levers to steer the 'train'. A bigger locomotive followed the next year and also went to Russia. It is stated to have worked on Russian rivers in the winter of 1861–62 hauling three ordinary railway carriages with sledges substituted for the wheels. At one time it provided a mail service between Kronstadt and St Petersburg. Later locomotives, sometimes with caterpillar treads instead of wheels, hauled lumber in Canada and the U.S.A. – a job taken over by the giant diesel tractors of today.

Quite recently, Mr. William H. Reinholz of the U.S.A. drew up plans for jet-propelled trains which would run at 300–500 m.p.h. in plastic tubes. There would be runners instead of wheels, and these would glide in twin channels filled with ice kept frozen by a plant using atomic energy. Many inventors have considered ways in which trains could be guided without

'Uniline' train on concrete track with centre guide rail.

having a railway or tram track to carry them. One of the principles they had in mind was to retain the easy rolling characteristics of the rail for the load but to use the friction produced by wheels running on a road. Thus we had systems like Larmanjat's, demonstrated in France from 1868 onwards, in which the cars ran on a single rail with lateral support from road wheels, but the locomotive had its main driving wheels and weight on the road with subsidiary wheels only to steer it along the track. A modern version of this, designed by Major F. Dutton, was demonstrated at the Wembley British Empire Exhibitions of 1924–25. This had twin rail track on which the vehicles ran, but the tractor had wheels running on prepared strips outside the rails.

After this came systems in which all the vehicles ran on pneumatic tyres but were guided by a single, non-load-carrying rail. One example of this was the 'Guideways' system tried out in India in the 1930s and subsequently refined and demonstrated as the 'Uniline' system in Sussex in the 1950s. Very similar ideas, with detail differences, have been proposed for buses, airport services, etc., many with the added proposition that the vehicles should be capable of being steered so that they could also run on ordinary roads – a proposition put forward, incidentally, by Richard Trevithick in the earliest days of mechanical traction. An advantage of the guided system is that it can run on a track, or track strips, just

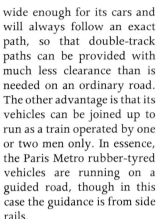

wide enough for its cars and will always follow an exact path, so that double-track paths can be provided with much less clearance than is needed on an ordinary road. The other advantage is that its vehicles can be joined up to run as a train operated by one or two men only. In essence, the Paris Metro rubber-tyred vehicles are running on a guided road, though in this case the guidance is from side rails.

In recent years a new type of vehicle has been invented which has virtually no friction drag at all. Known technically as a 'ground effect' vehicle, it is better known in Britain as the hovercraft. Though much of their development has been for use over water they are equally suitable for use over flat land and are potentially capable of high speeds. As at present under development, most ground effect vehicles, or cushion craft, depend on a fairly low-pressure cushion of air to keep them above the ground.

The idea now is to apply these craft to railway pur-

Model of high-speed monorail Levacar, with air-cushioned supporting and guiding slipper.

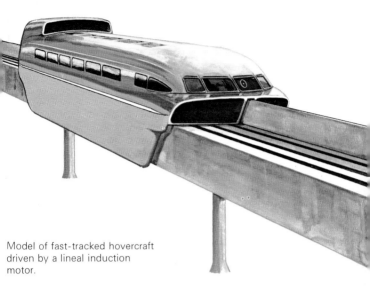

Model of fast-tracked hovercraft driven by a lineal induction motor.

poses, using a smooth track which will give the best characteristics for the air cushion and at the same time provide precise guidance. Mr Christopher Cockerell, generally regarded as the 'father' of the hovercraft, has put forward proposals for a tracked hovercraft which would seat 150 people and run on special track shaped to fit the underside of the vehicle, a half-inch air cushion giving the friction-free clearance needed for the car. Trains of cars could be used at low speeds, but for high speeds of up to 300 m.p.h. cars would run singly. A track was built, for high speed testing, but the British government withdrew support.

A rather similar scheme has been proposed by the Ford company with their Levacar project. This would use air-cushion vehicles running over prepared smooth surfaces – possibly twin surfaces looking rather like a conventional railway – but using high air pressures of up to 100 p.s.i. and having only a few thousandths of an inch clearance between rail and running gear. The principle is really more akin to air-lubricated bearings than air cushioning. Propulsion, by jet engines, would be at speeds of up to 500 m.p.h.

It is difficult to see how, in built-up countries, room could conveniently be found for long routes for either of these systems, but it might be possible to build them, at a price, above existing motorways or railways.

Yet another version of this idea has been tried very successfully in France. This is the Bertin aerotrain, which, in the prototype, has a small six-seat vehicle propelled by an aircraft engine. The concrete track is shaped like an inverted 'T', the base providing the flat surface needed by the air cushion and the central spine steering the car. The car can manoeuvre on rubber-tyred wheels when off the track or use them on the track at low speeds when noise must be reduced. The Bertin car, with rocket assistance, attained a speed of 233 m.p.h. on a trial circuit near Paris. The project had the backing of the French government.

For all vehicles of this type there is great promise in the linear induction motor now under development in several countries. Its principle is well known, and has been for many years, but efforts are now being directed to building it in a reasonably cheap but effective form. The linear motor is in effect a normal electric motor laid out flat, with the static part

of the motor producing a magnetic field which sweeps from one end to the other instead of moving round a circle as in an ordinary motor in which the field carries the rotor round with it. In the linear motor the 'rotor' is swept along in a straight line. When applied to a track, the 'rotor' portion can take the form of a steel or aluminium plate fixed permanently in position along the length of the whole track. There is no physical contact between one part of the motor and the other, and no friction. The power applied is independent of contact between the vehicle and track, so that full power can be applied without the usual wheel slip.

It might seem that the linear motor is ideal for ordinary railways with their lack of friction between wheel and rail, but experiments have shown that costs are much too high for low-speed work, and the linear motor does not come into its own below 150 m.p.h.

A possible alternative to an air cushion for frictionless movement is magnetic suspension, using repulsion magnets to lift a car a few inches. This has been suggested in the past but has been too expensive for any practical purpose, and

Bertin propeller-driven 'Aerotrain' supported on air cushion and guided by centre fin of track.

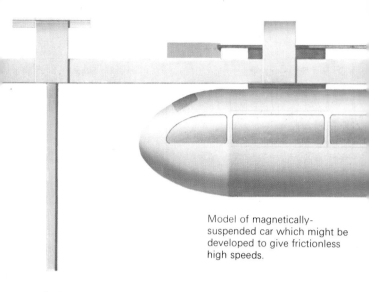

Model of magnetically-suspended car which might be developed to give frictionless high speeds.

electro-magnets have been essential. Now, with very powerful permanent magnets available from the development of ferrites, which are sintered ceramic materials based on ferric oxide, it would be possible to install opposing magnets in the track and in the car so as to achieve permanent flotation of the car without using energy. Such a system is the 'Magnarail' using magnets as described and propelling the car by a linear motor. Other similar systems are on trial. Braking in linear motored vehicles is accomplished by reversing the motor, setting up a drag which swiftly halts the car. In emergencies, cars could also drop friction skids on to the track.

For transport in towns, a number of small-capacity systems without rails have been suggested from time to time. One of the first of these was the 'Never-Stop' railway, which had no rails but ran with rubber-tyred wheels on two concrete strips. They were steered by horizontal wheels running on the inside edges of the strips and driven by a varying pitch spiral drive running between the tracks. This was arranged so that the turns of the spiral were close together in stations, so that the cars went through very slowly, giving plenty of time for passengers to get in and out. Between stations the pitch

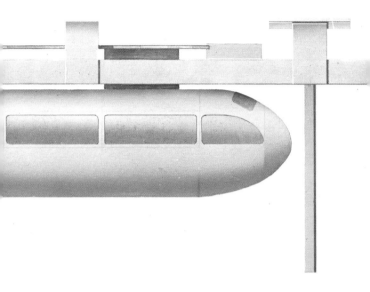

widened and the speed went up to 12 m.p.h. In more recent versions 36 m.p.h. can be reached. The 'Never-Stop' carried millions of people at the Wembley Exhibitions.

Among more recent systems is the 'staRRcar', or self-transit rail and road car. In this system the user can have the special small car overnight in his own garage. In the morning he drives off just as in a normal car until he reaches the nearest entrance to a staRRcar track. He enters this just as one would enter a motorway, and once the car is on the track its driving is taken over automatically. As it enters the main track from the approach spur it speeds up to 70 m.p.h. until it reaches the rear of a train of staRRcars ahead, when it slows to 60 m.p.h. and joins the train, being joined in its turn by other cars behind. The driver then punches a code on buttons on the dash to show which exit from the staRRcar system he wishes to take. When the time comes his car is automatically switched out of the train on to a decelerating lane, at the end of which he drives off in the normal way. For those who cannot drive, a car could be picked up at a staRRcar garage connected to the system and routed to the garage nearest the destination. StaRRcar tracks would normally be over existing roads.

Running on a trial line in Pittsburgh are small Westinghouse Electric rubber-tyred twenty-seat vehicles using a twin concrete surface track with a guide rail between. They are entirely automatic in operation and are controlled by a central computer. In slack hours they run singly but in peak hours can form trains of up to ten cars: these attractive vehicles are capable of 50 m.p.h. between stations. This 'Skybus' or 'Transit Expressway' is regarded as a promising low-cost rapid transit system for cities of medium size. This system, which, with two other developments, earned for Westinghouse the U.S. Department of Housing and Urban Development's first award for outstanding achievements in urban transportation development, has been adopted for Tampa airport and was considered in Baltimore for at least one rapid transit route.

For the last century-and-a-half, railways have risen, flourished, and apparently declined, only to have a second day. The economic magic of steel wheels on steel rails still holds good, as the new fast passenger and freight trains and the massive upsurge in urban mass transit testify. But the

'Skybus' rubber-tyred, rail-guided
automatic unmanned urban
train on trials in a Pittsburgh
park, U.S.A.

'ringing grooves of change' are still changing. The new technologies may eventually leave us with no more than the self-guiding characteristics of railways. If the new methods prove superior it is right that rails should give way to them, for it should never be forgotten that railways exist to carry passengers and goods, and not as an end in themselves.

But before the railways die it is likely that they will develop to heights as yet almost unsuspected. They may well have another century of life before them, maybe even more, because they can so readily accept the fruits of automation. The railwaymen who will man them in those days must be a far cry from those who ran the fledgling colliery railways of Northern England in the early nineteenth century. For railways all is change.

'You are not the same people who left that station
Or who will arrive at any terminus,
While the narrowing rails slide together behind you.'

T. S. ELIOT

MUSEUMS TO VISIT

In Britain

The Railway Museum, York.
The Great Western Railway Museum, Swindon.
The Science Museum, South Kensington.
The City of Belfast Transport Museum, Belfast 4.
The Birmingham Museum of Science and Industry.
The Newcastle Museum of Science and Engineering.
The London Transport Collection, Syon Park, Brentford.

In the U.S.A.

(This list is not comprehensive. There are many museums with transport exhibits in the U.S.A. and visitors should make enquiries locally.)
The Smithsonian Institution, Washington, D.C.
Chicago Museum of Science and Industry.
Colorado Railroad Museum, Golden, Colorado.
Ohio Railway Museum, Worthington, Ohio.
Henry Ford Museum, Dearborn, Michigan.
Museum of Transport, St Louis, Missouri.
'Steamtown U.S.A.', North Walpole, New Hampshire.
Benjamin Franklin Institute, Philadelphia, Pennsylvania.
Railroad Museum, Jackson, Tennessee.

The publishers wish to thank Faber and Faber Ltd and Harcourt, Brace & World, Inc. for permission to reprint the lines that appear on page 155 from T.S. Eliot's 'The Dry Salvages' from *The Four Quartets*.

BOOKS TO READ

British Railway History, Vol. I, 1830 to 1876, Vol. II, 1877 to 1947 by C. Hamilton Ellis. Allen & Unwin (USA : Hillary House), 1960.

The Railway Age by Michael Robbins. Routledge & Kegan Paul (Penguin Edition: 1965; US: Dufour Editions), 1962.

The Railway Engineers by O. S. Nock. B. T. Batsford, 1955.

Modern Railway Working by B. K. Cooper. Leonard Hill, 1957.

Modern Railways the World Over by G. Freeman Allen. Ian Allan.

Father of Railways by O. S. Nock. Thomas Nelson & Sons Ltd., 1958.

Isambard Kingdom Brunel by L. T. C. Rolt. Longmans, Green & Co. Ltd. (Grey Arrow paperback edition 1961), 1957.

Famous Railways of the World by B. G. Wilson and John R. Day. Frederick Muller. (Third [Revised] impression 1960).

Railway Signalling Systems by John R. Day and B. K. Cooper. Frederick Muller. (Second [Revised] edition 1963).

Railway Locomotives by John R. Day and B. K. Cooper. Frederick Muller, 1960.

Unusual Railways by John R. Day and B. G. Wilson. Frederick Muller. (USA : Macmillan) (Second [revised] impression 1960).

More Unusual Railways by John R. Day. Frederick Muller (USA : Macmillan), 1960.

Pictorial Encyclopedia of Railways by Hamilton Ellis. Paul Hamlyn, 1967.

Railways of Southern Africa by John R. Day. Arthur Barker (USA : Humanities Press), 1963.

Railways of Northern Africa by John R. Day. Arthur Barker (USA : Humanities Press), 1964.

Railways Under the Ground by John R. Day. Arthur Barker, 1964.

The Story of London's Underground by John R. Day. London Transport (Revised Edition 1974).

The Horizon Book of Railways by Various Authors. Paul Hamlyn, 1961.

Transport Today and Tomorrow by John R. Day, Peter Duff and Michael Hill. Lutterworth Press, 1967.

INDEX

Page numbers in **bold**
type refer to illustrations.

Aeolus 8
Aerotrain 150, **150–151**
Air-rail services 97, 145
American Civil War 32, **33**
Armoured train **33**,
  134–135, 135
Automatic door operation
  132
Automatic fare collection
  116, 120–123, **120–121**,
  130
Automatic train 116,
  122–123, 123, 126,
  129–130, 132–133, 142
Automatic warning 73

Ballast 55, **59**, 60
Baltimore & Ohio
  Railroad **7**, 8, 19
Bessemer, Sir Henry 54
Best Friend of Charleston
  12, 13
Blenkinsop, John **54**
Booth, Henry 12
Brakes 40, 65, 73, 82, 126
  electric 82, 126
  hydraulic 126
Brandreth, Thomas Shaw 6
Brassey, Thomas 15, 21
Brunel, I.K. 15, 16
British Railway 6, 40, 45,
  48, 49, **48–49**, 80,
  80–81, 126, **127**, 130
Broadway Limited 28
Burstall, Timothy 11

'Cape to Cairo' Railway 30
Capitole 38
Catch-me-who-can **8**, 9
Catenary 79
Catering 20, 27, 29, 99, **99**
Centralized traffic control
  62, 72, **72**
Central Pacific Railroad
  18, 21
Channel Tunnel **60–61**, 62
Chicago & Atlantic
  Railway **25**
City and South London
  Railway 113
Coal 4, 5, 11, 47, **47**, 48,
  100, **107**, 109, 111
Commuting 37–38, **40**,

41–43, 90, 92, **94**, 117,
  130–133
Compagnie Internationale
  des Wagons-Lits 28
Construction **14**, 15, 114,
  117–120, 125–126,
  128–130, 132–133
Container, refrigerated
  46, **108**, 109
Container services 45–50,
  53, **96–97**, 105, 106–107,
  109, 128, **128–129**
Cooper, Peter 13
Cyclopede 6, 11

Diesel, Rudolf 76
Diesel trains 28, **36**, 37, **44**,
  52, 83, 86, 102, 125, 142
Dixon, John 15
Dutton, Major F. 147

Electric trains 24, 25, 26,
  26, **27**, 35, 36, **38**,
  38–39, **41**, 62–65,
  78–84, 112–113, **113**,
  116, 125–126
Expresses 36, **36**, **37**, 38,
  39, **124–125**, 132

Ferry 60–61, **61**
Fletcher, Edward 15
Flying Scotsman 26
Freight 24, 40, 41, 44–53,
  44–45, 60, **61**, 84, 86,
  100–101, 100–111,
  128–130, **132–133**, 154
Freightliner **48–49**, 49, 50,
  105–106, 128, **128–129**
French National Railways
  83
Funicular railway 120,
  137–138, **138**

Gas-turbine engine
  86–87, **87**
Gauge
  broad 16, 17, 22, 142
  narrow **30**, 32, 142
  standard 5, 16, 17, 31,
  47, 135
Gauge Commission 16–17
Gooch, Daniel 16
Gray, Thomas 15
Great Northern Railway
  26, **44**

Great Western Railway
  15, 16, **21**, **23**
Gresley, Sir Nigel **33**, 74
Grew, Nathaniel 146

Hackworth, Timothy 11,
  12
Horse-drawn train 6,
  6–7, 11, 19, 22
Hovercraft 148, **149**,
  149–151
Hudson, George 17
Huskisson, William 13
Hydraulic drive train 78,
  84, 126

Illinois Central Railroad
  20
Inter-container 53
Invicta 15

James, William 15
Jessop, William 6, 54
Jet-propelled train 146,
  149

Kangarou trailer 47, **105**,
  109

Liverpool & Manchester
  Railway 11, 12, 15, **20**,
  21, 24, 43, 65, 67
Liverpool Street Station 41
Locke, Joseph 15
Locomotion **9**, 11
Locomotive
  diesel 36, **76–77**, 81, 82,
  83, 142
  electric **37**, 74–75, 78,
  80–81, **80–81**, 83
  steam 74, 75, 77
  turbine 39, 126, **127**
  wood-burning 24–25
London & Birmingham
  Railway 15
London & North Western
  Railway 26, 27
London & Southampton
  Railway 15
London Transport 91

Mail train 22, **42–43**, 43,
  87, 146

Mallard 74
Marshalling yard
   101–104, **103**, 104, 110
'Merry-go-round' train
   47, 48
Metropolitan Railway 23,
   112–113
Midland Railway 27
Military train 32, 134
Mistral 36, 38, **78**
Monorail 116, 139–141,
   140–141, 142, 143–144,
   143, 148
Multiple-unit train 43, 128
Münchner **13**
Mushet, R. F. 54

North British Railway 26
North Eastern Railway 26
Novelty 12

Orient Express 29

Passenger services 22, 24,
   26, 34–43, 44, 60, **61**,
   84, 86, 87, 97–99,
   98–99, 124, 128–129,
   133, 154
Perseverance 11
'Piggy-back' trailer **46**,
   47, **105**, 107
Pioneer Zephyr 28
Points 102, 104
Priestman, W. D. 76
Pullman car, **18–19**, **25**,
   27, 29
Pullman, George
   Mortimer 20, 27

Rack railway 136–137,
   139
Rail 54–63
   bullhead 56, 57
   cast-iron 6, 54
   flanged 9, **54**
   flat-bottom 57
   steel 54–55, 116, 124,
      154
   welded **55**, 57, 59
   wooden 5, 19
   wrought iron 54
Railway Bills 19
Rainhill Trials 6, **10**
Refrigeration 46, **108**, 109
Reinholz, William H, 146
Road-rail services **46**,
   52–53, 52, **86**, **104–105**,
   107–108, **108**

Rocket 6, **10**, 12, 13
Rocket power 135–136,
   136
Romanshorn **61**

Sacramento Valley
   Railroad 20
Sans Pareil 12
Sea-rail services 50, 96,
   96–97
Seguin, Marc 13
Shunting 43, 84, **85**, 86,
   101–104, **103**
Siding 102, 104, 105
Siemens, Werner von 24,
   26, 79
Signal
   coded 70–72, **71**
   colour-light **64**, 66, 69
   disc and crossbar **64**, 67
   flag 66, 67
   radar 130
   semaphore **64**, 67, 69
Signalbox **66–67**, 69
Signalling 40, 41, 42, 51,
   64, 65–73, 126,
   129–130, 132
Sleeper 6, 55–56, **55**, 57,
   59, 60
Sleeping facilities 20, 27, 29
South Carolina Railroad
   6, 9, 13, 19
Stage coach 31–32, 34
Station 88–99, **88**, **89**,
   94–95
Steam locomotive 6, 9,
   10, 11, **11**, 12, 13, 19,
   21, 24, 26, 28, 40,
   74–75, **75**, 78, 112, **112**,
   146
Stephenson, George 10,
   10, 11, 12, 15, 17, 22, 74
Stephenson, Robert 11,
   12, 15, 21, 22, 30
Stevens, Colonel John 13
Stirling locomotive **28**
Stockton & Darlington
   Railway 9, 11, 15
Stourbridge Lion 13
Stuart, Akroyd 76
Surrey Iron Railway 6
Suspension 124–125,
   151–152, **152**

Talgo train 141–142, **145**
Telegraph 21, 22, **23**, 67
Third rail system 78–80
Ticket 89–90, **90**, **91**, 92
Ticket machine,
   automatic 92, 121, 130

Timetable 23, 89
Tokaido Line 38–39, **39**,
   63, 125, 126, 128, 129
Tom Thumb 13
Track
   circuit **68**, 70, 142
   concrete 63, **63**, **146**,
      150, 152
   control 62, 72–73, **72**,
   laying **58**, 59–60
   maintenance **59**, 60,
      62–63
   single 146, **146**,
      147–148
Trailer, Kangarou 47, **105**,
   108
Trailer, Piggy-back **46**,
   47, **105**, 107
Trans-Australian
Trans-Europe Express 36,
   36, 53
Trans-Siberian Railway 29
Travelling Post Office
   42–43, 43
Trevithick, Richard **8**, 9,
   10, 147
Tunnel 30, 58, 61, 114, 125
   spiral **56**, 59
Tunnelling shield 114, **114**
*Twentieth Century
   Limited* 28
Tyre
   pneumatic 147
   rubber 116, **118**, **119**,
      120, 140, 148, 150, 152,
      154, **154**

Underground railway 16,
   42, 70, 73, **73**, 79–80,
   94, 112–123, **112**, **113**
Union Pacific Railroad **18**,
   21, 86, **87**

Volk, Magnus 26, **27**

Wagon 16, 47, **49**, 51,
   109, **110**
   hopper 48, **106–107**,
      109, 110
Wheel
   flanged 4, 9, **54**, 126
   rubber 140, 150, 152
   steel 116, 120, 124, 155
   toothed **54**, 136–137
Wilson, Robert 11

York & North Midland
   Railway 17